REFORM AND MARKET
DEMOCRACY

Reform and Market Democracy

George Macesich

PRAEGER

New York
Westport, Connecticut
London

Library of Congress Cataloging-in-Publication Data

Macesich, George, 1927–
    Reform and market democracy / George Macesich.
      p.   cm.
    Includes bibliographical references and index.
    ISBN 0-275-93989-8 (alk. paper)
    1. Europe, Eastern—Economic conditions—1989- 2. Mixed economy
—Europe, Eastern. 3. Capitalism—Europe, Eastern. 4. Democracy.
5. Nationalism—Europe, Eastern. 6. Right of property—Europe,
Eastern.   I. Title.
HC244.M224   1991
338.947—dc20   91-10179

British Library Cataloguing in Publication Data is available.

Library of Congress Catalog Card Number: 91-10179
ISBN: 0-275-93989-8

First published in 1991

Praeger Publishers, One Madison Avenue, New York, NY 10010
An imprint of Greenwood Publishing Group, Inc.

Printed in the United States of America

The paper used in this book complies with the
Permanent Paper Standard issued by the National
Information Standards Organization (Z39.48-1984).

10 9 8 7 6 5 4 3 2 1

For

S. S. M.

Maya, Milena, and George M. P.

Contents

Preface

This book serves to commemorate the thirtieth anniversary of the Center for Yugoslav-American Studies, Research, and Exchanges at Florida State University and its programs in comparative policy studies. It is an addition to a growing list of studies undertaken by the Center. These include recent studies such as *Essays on the Political Economy of Yugoslavia since 1974* (Rikard Lang, George Macesich, and Dragomir Vojnic, eds., 1982); *Money and Finance in Yugoslavia: A Comparative Analysis* (Dimitrije Dimitrijevic and George Macesich, 1984); *Essays on Comparative Managerial Practices in the U.S. and Yugoslavia* (Dan Voich and Mijat Damjanovic, eds., 1985); *Direct Foreign Investment in Yugoslavia: A Microeconomic Model* (T. Misha Sarkovic, 1986); *Dictionary of Yugoslav Political Economic Terminology* (English/Serbo-Croatian) (Vlasta Andrlic and Ljiljana Jovkovic, eds., 1985); *Essays on the Yugoslav Economic Model* (George Macesich, Rikard Lang, and Dragomir Vojnic, eds., 1989); and *Money Supply Process* (Dimitrije Dimitrijevic and George Macesich, 1991).

This study argues that market democracy offers an organizing principle for reform to Eastern European and other countries currently searching for a model on which to base their drive to a market economy.

Market democracy is the culmination of more than three hundred years of economic and political thought. It is centered on a theory of pluralistic democracy in a free market–oriented society with private property and civil rights transcending narrow nationalism, where everyone has the freedom to develop. It does not share the Marxist pretension that commandeering society is the one way to assure prosperity and freedom. It is equally skeptical of the nationalism that has replaced Marxism in many of these countries as the guiding spirit of government.

An organizing principle for reform is important. It serves as a guide for people to think about a political economy. Without such a principle, the state will again become dominant. The political and economic structure will be taken over by well-organized special interests to the detriment of the rest of society. Reform will simply serve to perpetuate the interests of the ever-active political elite and the bureaucracy.

There are many lessons of successful reform. At least two, however, should be underscored. One is that all the elements of a well-designed reform program are interdependent, mutually supporting, and interactive. It is folly to focus on one or another of the elements in the program to the exclusion of the rest. Another lesson is that speed is essential. The total program may well take years to carry through before the benefits become visible. The costs, however, appear immediately. Move too slowly and the consensus that supports the reform can collapse. It is uncertainty, not speed, that endangers a reform program and casts doubt on the government's credibility to carry it out.

Nationalism can be an important force in reform and national renewal. Unfortunately, its negative side is likely to subvert reform and market democracy. In particular, the kind of nationalism arising in Eastern and Central Europe, with undertones of jealousy, rivalry, and exclusion, will not support the compromise and tolerance that market democracy requires. This study draws on the experience of the Austro-Hungarian Empire as a case in point, demonstrating the futility of promoting narrow nationalism in the ethnic hodgepodge that constitutes the population in this part of Europe. Yugoslavia's recent experience reinforces that of Austro-Hungary, as does that of the Soviet Union.

The former ruling Marxist ideology clearly failed to encourage people in this area of Europe to work their way through the gradual accommodation that brought other Europeans to realize that they must live harmoniously together. Strengthening a sense of nationalism thus becomes another catch-up job for these countries, along with all of the other serious problems before them. However, it will make solutions to all the other problems even more difficult if it is not done properly.

I am indebted to many colleagues with whom I have discussed one or another aspect of this study over the years. These include Marshall R. Colberg, Walter Macesich, Jr., Milton Friedman, Anna J. Schwartz, Dragomir Vojnic, Rikard Lang, Ljubisav Markovic, Ljubisa Adamovic, and Dimitrije Dimitrijevic. I would like to express appreciation to Mrs. Esther C. S. Glenn, editor at the Center for Yugoslav-American Studies, Research, and Exchanges, for her efficient and helpful editing of the manuscript; and to Mrs. Beverly McNeil, secretary to the Center, for her word processing.

1

Organizing Market Democracy

AN ORGANIZING PRINCIPLE

This study focuses on market democracy, which is taken to mean a pluralistic democracy in a free market-oriented society with private property and civil rights, transcending narrow nationalism, where everyone has the freedom to develop. It stands in marked contrast to socialism, which is defined as the organization of society in which the means of production of goods and services are not in private hands. It differs from the narrow capitalism of Marxism by incorporating more than three hundred years of experience with economic and political reform.

Judging from recent world experience, a socialist society—particularly the type recently in place in Eastern European countries—has not been as successful in producing the quantity and quality of goods and services as a market democracy organized on the principles of a private free market and private ownership of the means of production. Market democracy not only produces more than a socialist society, but it also allows individuals more liberty to chose how, where, when, and for whom they will use their productive services.

Moreover, there is good reason to believe that the figures on the total output of goods and services produced in the socialist economies of Eastern Europe and the Soviet Union have been inflated by (1) double counting of inputs, (2) inadequate depreciation allowances, (3) inclusion of wasted materials, and (4) understatement of inflation. Repressed inflation results in waiting lines and a lack of goods at official prices.

As these countries move toward market systems and as excess demand is eliminated by price increases that reflect market supply and demand (which, ironically, reduce real wages), the standard of living does not necessarily decline. Indeed, in a shortage economy a drop in real wages can mean the elimination of waiting lines and a rise in living standards. The time saved in not standing in long lines should also be considered.

It is for these reasons that economists are now putting forth new concepts and methods to measure the standard of living. They include factors such as the degrees of well-being and freedom that people experience in their day-to-day living. The standard of living is more than a basket of goods and services that people can afford to buy by working for a specified period of time. Living in a polluted environment, for instance, does not raise a person's standard of living even if he can afford to purchase more material goods and services.

The quest for higher living standards is ultimately linked to the desire for freedom; each is really an aspect of the other. When people lack the capability to choose how to get or spend income, their standard of living is diminished. Attempts by Marxist and authoritarian governments to improve economic performance by expanding the role of the market while tightly restricting political freedom constitute a contradiction in terms that undermines living standards and is ultimately self-defeating. The recent history of Eastern Europe and the Soviet Union suggests that a people's determination to achieve a higher standard of living underlies the drive not only for better economic performance but for political freedom and democracy as well. These are desires that a market democracy can satisfy.

Market democracy thus stands in marked contrast to the doctrines followed by the Communist party in the Soviet Union and elsewhere that include (1) the predominance of class interest, (2) the monopoly of one party, and (3) full state control of the economy. It does not share the Marxist pretension that commandeering society is the one way to assure prosperity and freedom. It is equally skeptical of the nationalism that has replaced Marxism in many of these countries as the guiding spirit of government. For its part, this study discusses the economic implications of nationalism. It recognizes that attempts to push nationalism back into history have not been successful. For more than two centuries nationalism has been the mainspring of history. Indeed, the power of nationalism to move events appears stronger than that of other "isms," including Marxism. Its emotions have not lost their power over the years. One astute scholar put the issue succinctly when he argued that a nation is a people united by a common dislike of its neighbors and by a common mistake about its origins.

The lesson is that while nations can be made more or less democratic and rich, they cannot be made at all without nationalism. It may well be that as societies and economies evolve, nationalism may place more emphasis on the preservation of social and cultural distinctiveness than the often murderous preservation of political claims. Whatever the course, the power of nationalism should not be underestimated. The Victorian conviction that everything is inevitably for the better may well be subject to qualification in the case of nationalism.

Market democracy can serve as an organizing principle for people to think about a political economy. This is important, for without an organizing principle, the state will become dominant. Professor James Buchanan puts the problem succinctly when he writes:

With no overriding principle that dictates how an economy is to be organized, the political structure is open to exploitation by the pressures of well-organized interests. The special-interest, rent-seeking, churning state finds fertile ground for growth in this environment. And, depending on the relative strength of organized interests, we observe quite arbitrary, politicized interferences with markets.[1]

For these reasons (among others), Professor Buchanan calls attention to the need for constitutional constraints to prevent the least desirable outcomes of majoritarian democratic processes and to guarantee a depoliticized economic order. Such constraints are necessary for the success of a market democracy.[2]

KEY ROLE OF PRICES AND MARKETS

Consider the role of prices and markets, which are key elements in a market democracy. In his book *Economic Organization*, Frank Knight points out that the economic problem may be broken down into five interrelated problems.[3] Provisions must be made by every society for handling these five problems: (1) fixing standards, (2) organizing production, (3) distributing the product, (4) providing for economic maintenance, and (5) adjusting consumption to production over short periods.

The existence of alternative ends implies that there must be some way of setting priorities among these ends and resolving conflicting evaluations by individuals within a society. In a free-market economy, this problem is resolved by voting in the market place with money. Such an arrangement amounts to proportional representation and allows economic minority groups within society to make their desires known. These votes in the free-market economy manifest themselves through prices that, in turn, reflect the standards of society.

Translation of these standards into production among and within industries again involves prices. The task is accomplished by the interaction of two sets of prices: the price of products and the price of resources. Prices of products in relation to their production costs determine the distribution of inputs among industries; the relative prices of input factors, in turn, determine the coordination of these factors within industries.

The means to divide the total product must be established by every society. In a society incorporating the free-market economy, this task is accomplished by the price system. Under such an arrangement separate individuals in a society own the means used in production. They get a claim on society's product by selling services on the market for a price. An individual's total claim on the product is determined by the quantity of resources he has and by the prices at which he can sell all the services of these resources. The return per unit of type of resource or input-factor prices in conjunction with the distribution of ownership of resources determines the distribution of the total product among individuals and society.

In effect, prices serve as signals indicating where economic resources are wanted most. At the same time, they produce an incentive for people to obey these signals. Because factor prices serve the function of distributing the product, other prices—mainly product prices—can serve the functions of fixing standards and organizing production.

The first three problems identified in this section deal with the adjustment of production to consumption. The organization of existing resources and their utilization in known ways are the only economic problems a static society need concern itself with. In a changing society, however, problems affecting the volume of resources and changes in their utilization require solutions. This is the fourth problem on our list, and it concerns economic maintenance and progress. In a free-market economy, the relevant price for solving this problem is the interest rate, which is an incentive for owners of capital to maintain their capital or to add to it. Here, the individual consumer has a voice in decisions affecting economic growth by his choice of saving. Some provision must be made for the quick adjustment of relatively fixed supplies of a commodity to consumption (the fifth problem). Bribery, chance, favoritism, or prices are among the means available to society to accomplish this task. When free bidding for goods is permitted, prices will adjust themselves so that the quantity people want to buy at the market price is equal to the quantity available.

In solving our five problems, prices do three things: (1) They transmit information effectively and efficiently; (2) they provide an incentive to users of resources to follow such information; and (3) they provide an incentive to owners of resources to follow this information.

This summary of the role of prices in a free-market economy is a brief and oversimplified version of an extremely subtle and highly complex procedure. The complexities are driven home only when something goes wrong or when attempts are made to find substitute methods for solving the five interrelated problems.

THE PRICE SYSTEM AND ECONOMIC DEVELOPMENT

Criticism of the price system on the grounds that it cannot achieve economic development rests on the relevance of external economies and complementarities.[4] According to this argument, private and social benefits differ when economies are external to the firm and the industry. Where complementary factors and facilities are lacking, economic development is arrested. Industry, for example, is slow to take advantage of relatively low wages when complementary facilities are virtually nonexistent.

Whereas the argument that the price system cannot achieve rapid economic development rests on the existence of external economies, the argument that it will not do so rests on the existence of internal economies and monopoly.[5] For successful operation the price system requires effective competition as an energy source. Otherwise the economy rests on dead center, with private enterprise and the price system making little economic progress.

Along with these arguments is another one that shows the divergence between private and social costs and the existence of external diseconomies.[6] According to this argument, private individuals may be willing to develop a country's natural resources only if they can appropriate the capital represented by these resources.

In defense of the price system, the advantages most often cited—at least in well-developed economies—are in (1) capital formation, (2) dispersal of decisions, (3) risk, and (4) the incentive to innovate.[7] The private entrepreneur usually makes a better collector for capital formation than does the government. Because there is considerable uncertainty as to the exact nature of the bottlenecks that impede economic development, it makes little sense to allocate all of one's resources to a single goal, which may be unprofitable in the final analysis. New methods and ideas seldom receive a favorable audience in bureaucracies, where there is a tendency to dodge responsibility and cling to old methods and ideas.

As an economy develops and as resources acquire the mobility to allow demand and supply elasticities to become more pronounced, the price system will operate more smoothly; this enables marginal and structural changes to occur within the economy. People with a singular distrust of price mechanism operations may fail to take advantage of the mechanism's contribution as a delicate integrator of complex economic events. The net effect may be a serious slowdown of economic development.

Implicit in the argument of low supply elasticity is the questionable assertion that people in these countries tend to be less aware of alternative opportunities. If so, steps should be taken to improve the market's operation through better information instead of turning to an elaborate planning structure until the elasticities become larger.

Rigid central planners and critics of the price system have overstated their case about external diseconomies and complementarities. For example, early work by Ronald H. Coase suggests possible solutions to these vexing problems within the price system.[8] James M. Buchanan's work indicates that imperfections arising from political attempts to solve these problems may outweigh the economic benefits.[9] Moreover, viewing the world as though it were composed primarily of complements has serious methodological drawbacks.[10]

MONEY AND THE MONETARY SYSTEM

Nowhere is the need for constraints against undesired outcomes of majoritarian democratic processes more evident than in the exercise of monetary policy. Past monetary policies have been a major cause of economic instability throughout the world. A contributing factor to the poor performance of monetary policy is the ease with which money slips into the political arena to become a singularly important political issue. Discretionary authority facilitates monetary manipulation for political ends, thereby increasing uncertainty and casting in doubt money, the monetary system, and the monetary authority itself. This raises fundamental questions regarding public policy constraints in the monetary system, as well as the ideas and economic philosophy underlying past and current monetary policies.

This study considers money and, specifically, the quantity theory of money within the framework of the organizing principle of market democracy.

In order to be successful, market democracy must incorporate into its monetary arrangements a well-implemented and well-executed monetarist rule, which will serve to constrain money and the monetary system within a defined, nondiscretionary, and lawful policy system. Money and monetary theory are ideologically neutral. Of course, this does not mean that the situation must be the same in all countries or throughout history, although the evidence put forward by Milton Friedman and Anna J. Schwartz supports the view that money does indeed matter.[11]

NOTES

1. James Buchanan, "Socialism Is Dead: Leviathan Lives," *Wall Street Journal* (July 18, 1990), p. A10.

2. See also George Macesich, *Money and Democracy* (New York: Praeger, 1990); and George Macesich, ed., with the assistance of R. Lang, L. Markovic, and D. Vojnic, *Yugoslavia in the Age of Democracy: Essays on Economic and Political Reform* (Praeger, forthcoming).

3. Frank Knight, *Economic Organization* (Chicago: University of Chicago Press, 1933). See also Milton Friedman's "Lectures in Price Theory" (mimeographed, University of Chicago, 1955).

4. Charles P. Kindleberger, *Economic Development* (New York: McGraw-Hill, 1958), p. 132.

5. See Kindleberger, *Economic Development*, p. 133.

6. See Kindleberger, *Economic Development*, p. 133.

7. See Kindleberger, *Economic Development*, p. 134.

8. Ronald H. Coase, "The Problem of Social Cost," *Journal of Law and Economics* (October 1960), pp. 1–44.

9. James M. Buchanan, "Politics, Policy and the Pigovian Margins," *Economics* (February 1962), pp. 17–24.

10. George Macesich, "Current Inflation Theory: Consideration of Methodology," *Social Research* (Autumn 1961), pp. 321–30.

11. Milton Friedman and Anna J. Schwartz, *Monetary History of the United States, 1867–1960* (Princeton: Princeton University Press, for National Bureau of Economic Research, 1963); Milton Friedman and Anna J. Schwartz, *Monetary Trends in the United States and United Kingdom: Their Relation to Revenue, Prices, and Interest Rates, 1867—1975* (Chicago: University of Chicago Press, 1982).

---------- 2 ----------

Historical and Theoretical
Underpinnings

EARLY CONTRIBUTIONS

In 1848 Karl Marx wrote of the specter of communism haunting
Europe. In the closing years of the twentieth century, the Red
Specter has turned gray, and Europe surges on a wave of
democratic, market-oriented reforms. Evidently it pays to cultivate and subscribe to the organizing principle of market democracy.

This should not surprise us. Many contemporary issues of
government interaction and competition—as well as economic
and political reform—have been set for more than three hundred
years by a school of thought that arose to cope with the problems
of England in the period of great change following the seventeenth
century. The contributions of the thinkers of that era, particularly
to economic thought, are notable and deserve serious study. The
brief survey presented in this chapter suggests the importance of
their contributions to our study of market democracy.[1]

The organizing principle of market democracy, which appears
to correspond best to human nature and accommodates
humanity's heterogeneity, is the product of more than three
hundred years of economic and political thought. John Locke

(1632–1704) prepared the way for a scientific study of political economy when he set forth his exposition of a society based on natural rights of individuals. Among these rights property loomed large; Locke was a philosopher of the middle-class revolution of 1688. He represented the views of men who founded the Bank of England in 1694. The fight against the divine right of kings was won, and a new social order was dominated by the right of individual property. The connection between money and output—important for market democracy—received examination at the beginning of the eighteenth century. In addition to that of John Locke, the most outstanding contribution was made by John Law (1671–1729). In essence, Locke and Law focused on the obvious fact that total monetary receipts must equal total monetary payments. They contended that increases in the quantity of money and the velocity of circulation not only raised prices but expanded output. Their policy prescription was to increase the quantity of money. Their presentation of policies was designed to create a favorable balance of trade.

Richard Cantillon (1697–1734) focused on the processes by which variations in the quantity of money lead to variations in prices and output, thereby providing useful insights into monetary dynamics. He also recognized what others would later point out—that the nominal quantity of money is beneficial to trade only during the period in which it is actually increasing. Once a new equilibrium is reached, output will return to its original level at a higher price level. This process of increasing the quantity of money, however, cannot last indefinitely because the process leads to an adverse balance of payments and an outflow of money. How to buy the benefits of the inflationary process without generating balance-of-payment problems is a familiar issue in contemporary society.[2]

In the 1760s David Hume (1711–1776) linked the general level of prices to the quantity of money in the now-classic quantity theory of money and the theory of the price-specie flow mechanism of international trade. The larger the supply of money, argued Hume, the higher the price level was likely to rise; higher prices, in turn, tended to make exports less competitive in foreign markets and imports more competitive in home markets. A drive to enlarge the supply of money would be self-defeating because the accumulation of specie (gold and silver) would produce effects that would later erode the favorable balance of trade. Moreover, attempts to check such deterioration in the balance of trade by controls of one kind or another would be damaging to the national interest: It would deprive the country of the benefits of international specialization and division of labor.[3]

Henry Thornton (1760-1815), in *An Inquiry into the Nature and Effects of the Paper Credit of Great Britain 1802*, dealt with the same general topic Hume had treated in his monetary policy theories. However, Thornton considered not gold and silver but bank credit, by which he meant bank notes. These were the main circulating medium of value in Britain in his time.[4]

England was the center and testing ground for many of the ideas put forward by economists. In economic theory (as distinct from economic policy) the classical doctrine steadily won its way, especially in the United States, although it had essentially the same character as English commerce. As we will see, continental European preoccupations with economic strategy, misgivings about the moral consequences of the enterprise, historical criticism of economic institutions, and socialist theories of more equitable distribution and more humanistic production did not provide a fertile ground for English ideas.

Indeed, Walter Bagehot (1826-1877) of *The Economist* put it well when he was driven to explain the "obvious reasons why English political economy should thus be unpopular out of England." His explanation has two parts: In effect, it is difficult for most people to understand that political economy is an abstract science; moreover, it is particularly difficult for those whose economic development is less developed and more remote from the assumptions of a political economy than the English.[5]

Although they were rigorous and complete within the assumptions of their theory, many English writers excluded important aspects of economic policy that had been clearly revealed in earlier thought and that have never ceased to be influential in practice.[6] In addition, they did not make allowances for ethical considerations or the complexities of international politics. For them, social policy—particularly the welfare of general workers—although not ignored, did not represent any special problems to society. The controversial issues of past and contemporary economic policy arose largely from these ethical, political, and social factors.

Certainly, by the second half of the nineteenth century concern focused on the economic, social, and political problems cast up by rapidly industrializing European and American societies. Early in the twentieth century, most of the elements of the interventionist economic position, which John M. Keynes articulated later in theory, were in practice. How revolutionary the Keynesian revolution was in this is suggested in the brief survey presented in this chapter.

CLASSICAL CONTRIBUTIONS

The moral dilemma between individual and social benefits, which social philosophers and moralists wrestled with, was resolved by Adam Smith in his analysis of the market economy. His system of natural liberty, free markets, free men, and competition lead to an orderly increase in wealth of the nation. The free competitive play of individual selfishness was shown by Smith to be the source of economic growth, social order, and general welfare. In his view, individualism does not lead to chaos but to order and prosperity.

Smith did more. In The Wealth of Nations (1776), he provided economics with an analytical framework. The idea is of a competitive, self-adjusting market equilibrium following a path of growth and affluence.

At the same time, The Wealth of Nations was a philosophical treatise concerned with fundamental problems of order and chaos in human society. Smith provided what came to be, especially in England and the United States, the orthodox approach to economic problems and policy—one that is very much alive in the twentieth century.

Critics seize two limitations to Smith's analysis of the free market. One is the distribution of income, which, if highly unequal, will signal the market to provide more for the rich and little for the poor. If the distribution of income is wrong, production also will be wrong, however efficiently the market works to produce the goods and services. It is this very problem, in fact, that the early socialists raised and that Karl Marx (1818–1883) later developed into a theory about the breakdown of capitalism.

The second criticism, which is closely related to the issue of economic justice, concerns private property in land and capital. Smith's support for the institution of private property, as both natural and necessary to the preservation of economic incentives, is good liberal doctrine. The fact is, however, that he supports it only in advanced societies. In primitive societies, only labor is considered a factor of production to be rewarded by wages. Conversely, in advanced societies rent on land and profit on capital are also part of the costs of production. Since rent and profit as costs of production are really the products of social organization, not natural phenomena like human labor and the self-interest motive, Smith's idea of an equilibrium of natural forces in the market is compromised.[7]

These shortfalls provide socialists and others with an opening to argue that only a return to labor is natural. Accordingly, only when the full value of output is gained by labor through social ownership of the means of production (land and capital) would the natural state of society be regained. Economic justice would be served because the entire product of society would go to its producers, and society's demand would not be distorted by unearned income.

Thomas R. Malthus (1766–1834), David Ricardo (1772–1823), Jeremy Bentham (1748–1832), and Jean-Baptiste Say (1767–1832) contributed enormously to the body of ideas now called classical economics. Writing at the close of the eighteenth century and during the turbulent early years of the nineteenth century, they promoted economics to a "science." These were the years of political, social, and technological revolutions that wiped away the vestiges of feudalism and the old aristocratic order. Much was expected of the American and French revolutions by English intellectuals and others. Some attribute the success of the American Revolution to the support of English liberals. Political reform in England was at the time a pressing issue; even the French Revolution was looked upon favorably because it would bring democracy to France and peace to both countries.

The disappointment was great when the wars with France began and continued for almost two decades. The Napoleonic period dashed all hopes for liberal political reforms in England. The establishment concerned itself with holding the line and rooting out the "radicals." In 1795 the Habeas Corpus Act was suspended for five years; in 1799 the Anti-Combination Laws, which prohibited any combination of workers or employers, were instituted to regulate employment conditions. For the most part these laws were directed and enforced more against labor than against management; suppression ruled these turbulent years.

Nevertheless, problems created by the rapid changes brought about by the war years demanded attention. The most obvious problem concerned the growing number of poor displaced by the economic, political, and social turmoil of the period. This occurred because of (1) demobilization following the Napoleonic wars, and (2) the enclosures of common land, which displaced many farmers from their small plots. These factors only served to promote the growth of cities that were already overburdened with problems of poverty. Reaction against the French Revolution made it certain that the problems of the poor would receive little priority from conservative policymakers, particularly if solutions required political and social reforms. Still, something had to be done.

A solution was presented by a religious minister, Thomas Robert Malthus. His solution was consistent with the preservation of the status quo and called for minimal government intervention. Government, argued Malthus, can do little in any case because the problem of the poor is moral. The problem has its origins in two propositions: One is in the food supply; the other is in the sexual proclivities of man. The result is the Malthusian principle that "the power of population is infinitely greater than the power in the earth to produce subsistence for man."[8]

In effect, "misery and vice" hold population in check. If the supply of food increases, there is a corresponding increase in population until the food supply is brought back to subsistence level, which will stop the population increase. Wages tend toward the subsistence level, which is the natural wage. Any increase in wages above the natural or subsistence level causes the population to grow and wages to decline. If, on the other hand, the price of food increases, wages would be forced up to maintain the subsistence wage. Moreover, increasing relief to the poor would mean taking resources out of the hands of those willing to invest, thus decreasing output.

The implications for the poor are ominous. Relief payment simply raises the wages of the poor above subsistence and results in more people. No increase in food production takes place as poverty continues unabated. This is not a very happy state of affairs, but one for which the government and the conservative establishment are not to blame. Nature must be allowed to take its course.

For David Ricardo, capital accumulation is the mainspring of growth. Economic policy should be directed toward facilitating and promoting such accumulations. His model is based on the belief that economic freedom leads to maximum profits, the source of investment capital, and—in a competitive economy—profit-maximizing investments. Business is to be encouraged because it leads to maximum economic growth.

The political and social issues in England following the Napoleonic wars pivoted on whether the country should become more heavily industrialized or should preserve a balance with agriculture. The issues involved the role of England's landed aristocracy in the country's social and political system. The contest was drawn in Parliament on the so-called Corn Laws and the import of grain into England. Existing laws protected English agriculture against foreign competition without simultaneous significant increases in food prices.

As a result of war-created increases in demand for agricultural products, English farmers enjoyed considerable prosperity. When peace finally came, the farmers and landed interests pushed for the enforcement of the Corn Laws to preserve their prosperity. All sorts of schemes were advanced to promote agriculture as England's leading industry.

All of this was anathema to the English business community as it witnessed high food prices and high wages, reduced profits, and decreased exports—which spelled general ruin for England's industry. In turn, it demanded nothing less than the repeal of the Corn Laws. Ricardo and other economists entered the debate on the side of business interests and against those of agriculture. Ricardo argued that the landowners, not the farmers, benefit if the price of wheat is raised by tariffs. The high price of wheat enables an extension of the land under cultivation, which would not normally be profitable. However, the result in the older wheat-growing areas would be that landowners would raise rents to take advantage of the higher prices received by farmers. Consequently, a larger proportion of the nation's income would go to the landowners, who would use these additional resources not for productive investment but for luxury expenditures.

Moreover, additional capital and labor would be drawn from industry to enlarge agricultural production stimulated by artificially high food prices. The net result would be to distort the nation's productive pattern, retarding the country's natural development of industry. Ricardo noted that high food prices would require high wages and, thus, high costs of production in industry. Since England must sell the products of industry throughout the world, higher costs would reduce business for English exports and so reduce the level of output of industry. Profits would be reduced, thereby slowing capital accumulation and economic growth from a lack of incentive and investment resources.

If left alone, a country's economy will achieve the maximum growth possible, according to Ricardo. It is, therefore, important that business be left alone to pursue profits; thus, the nation would maximize the amount of savings and capital accumulation that are so necessary for growth. Government intervention would simply make the process of saving and accumulation all the more difficult. In effect, Ricardo reinforced the theoretical and ideological underpinnings set in place by Adam Smith. Business interests are indeed well served by Ricardo's analysis.

The facility with which the international economy is integrated into Ricardo's model served to reduce all economic phenomena to fundamental relationships among factors of production. It demonstrates that the international division and specialization of labor is advantageous to all nations and that protection of domestic producers serves simply to damage the country imposing such protection. Free trade is beneficial internationally as well as domestically. The famous law of comparative advantage is used in support of the free trade doctrine. Moreover, capital will seek out countries where the returns are highest, provided such nations assure political stability and offer protection for private property rights. All of this remains very much a part of contemporary international trade theory, if not practice.

The realization of the full benefits of free international trade helped to forge a sound international monetary and financial system. Ricardo insisted that the domestic monetary system be regulated to minimize any disruption in the international division of labor. He adopted a "bullionist" position, arguing that the domestic money supply should be directly tied to the country's gold supply. Such an arrangement guarantees that a country suffering from loss of gold through an unfavorable balance of trade automatically contracts its paper note issue. Contraction in the money supply tends to depress the country's general level of prices; this, in turn, encourages the desired adjustment in international accounts. The deficit country's exports become more attractive to foreigners while imports compete less successfully in home markets as the price of home-produced items declines. Ricardo, in effect, set out the essentials of the classical theory of the gold standard.

The idea that money used as a standard of value consists of bank notes redeemable in specie or bullion and that coins circulate at their value as bullion is central to the body of classical monetary ideas. This money is assumed to be convertible into gold or silver bars and to be freely exchangeable either as coin or as bullion between countries. Its value is fixed at its bullion value, and the rate of exchange between two currencies is easily calculated by comparing the intrinsic value of the precious metals, which would automatically adjust to the "needs of trade" in each country.

Moreover, there is nothing that governments can do about this. If they issued paper money beyond the amount that the public would accept in the belief that these notes could at any moment be converted into gold, the surplus issue would be cashed and the government would have to redeem it with gold and silver from its reserves. If the notes were made inconvertible, their values would fall and the price of gold—indeed, of all commodities—as measured in the paper money, would rise in proportion to their over-issue. This was Ricardo's argument in his pamphlet *The High Rise of Bullion: A Proof of the Depreciation of Bank Notes* (1810).9

The conclusion drawn by classical theorists is that governments must accept that the only true money (gold and silver, or specie) is beyond their control. All the elaborate government devices for increasing national supplies of specie are self-defeating. Money accommodates itself to the "needs of trade." If governments issue inferior monetary substitutes, their value will depreciate. There is no place, therefore, in classical theory for discretionary, interventionist monetary policies designed to maintain full employment, and balance-of-payments equilibrium or to combat inflation or depression.

It remained to be demonstrated that a free market would also achieve full employment of all resources including labor and capital. This appears to be demonstrated by Jean-Baptiste Say (1767–1832) in his *Treatise on Political Economy* (1803). The principle is Say's Law of Markets. According to Say, there can never be a general deficiency of demand or a glut of commodities throughout the economy. While there may be given sectors or industries in which over production may occur (along with a shortage in others), this is only a temporary situation. The fall in prices in one area and their rise in other areas will provide incentives for businessmen to shift production and thereby correct the situation.

Say pointed out that people produce in order to exchange their products for other products. Production thus creates its own demand. In general, it is therefore impossible for production to outrun demand. Say's Law of Markets dominated economic thought on the level of economic activity until the concept was challenged by J. M. Keynes in the 1930s.[10]

Jeremy Bentham (1748–1832) and "philosophical radicals" such as James Mill, David Ricardo, and John Stuart Mill agitated for political reform, democratic government, and majority rule. The utilitarian political philosophy that dominated the radicals' thinking called for nothing less than a social system based upon full democratic participation and majority rule. According to Bentham and his utilitarian followers, this was the only way that a social system could maximize its total welfare and distribute it as widely as possible.

Bentham differed significantly from the classical liberalism of the eighteenth century that emphasized individual freedom as the goal of public policy. He saw potential conflict in the idea that only individual action can create welfare. It is possible that the action of one person in pursuit of his own interest may injure another and so reduce his welfare. After all, argued Bentham, human society is organized by man-made institutional arrangements. Conscious action can create social reforms that enable men to live better. In effect, classical liberalism establishes through Benthamite utilitarianism a place for interventionist liberalism emphasizing social welfare. It is intervention and reform justified in terms of individual and social welfare and the "greatest good for the greatest number."[11]

Thanks to Benthamite ideas, economics could henceforth easily incorporate the most laissez-faire individualist as well as the most thoroughgoing social reformer.[12] The analytical apparatus is the same for both. Important differences arise from the assumptions and conclusions that each reaches. This is an attribute that economists preserve to the present time.

All was not well in the post-Napoleonic world. The French Revolution did not bring forth "liberty, equality, and fraternity," nor did the rapid economic and technological advance, usually called the Industrial Revolution, abolish poverty. Indeed, the post-Napoleonic reaction and repression and the re-establishment of old political, social, and economic privileges served to increase poverty and arrest democratic advances for the general public. Critics seized upon the observed inequalities to push from theory to practice an alternative vision of (1) society based on the cooperative element in man's nature, rather than the materialistic profit motive of private capitalism, and (2) egalitarianism in place of the unequal distribution of income that prevailed at the time. To these early socialist critics, society was an organic whole composed of classes, rather than independent individuals, as held by classical economists. The roots of modern socialism can be found in the post-Napoleonic Europe nurtured by reaction against economic and political circumstances of the era.

Private property and private ownership of the means of production, argued the socialists, constituted the root cause of the failure of the two great revolutions to abolish poverty and to create a political order of full democracy. A few owners of capital benefited from these social and technological revolutions, but the majority of people remained mired in poverty. The socialists called for abolishment of private property and privilege as a first step toward a new society of greater opportunity and dignity for all people.

The humanitarian and idealistic roots of early socialism are typified in the work and writings of Robert Owen (1771–1858).

His attempts in England and the United States to establish cooperative communities characterized by commonly owned land and worker-owned enterprises (where profit was not permitted) were not particularly successful. This is not surprising; individualism dominated the era.[13]

Unlike the utopian reformers, Karl Marx (1818–1883) coupled scholarship with revolutionary agitation. It was not enough, according to Marx, to theorize; one must build a revolutionary party capable of seizing power when capitalism collapses. He did not suffer lightly other socialists who happened to disagree with his views. In fact, he established the practice of vitriolic denunciation of opposing views that burdens so much of contemporary socialist literature.

In Marx's view, capitalism, which is a term he invented, is doomed. His demonstration of its demise drew upon so-called laws of motion of capitalist society. On one level Marx based his argument on the inherent injustices of capitalism that lead ultimately to economic and social conditions that cannot be maintained. At another level his argument was sociological in that class conflict between increasingly affluent capitalists and an increasingly miserable working class will erupt into social revolution. At still another level, the argument is economic with (1) the accumulation of capital in private hands, and (2) the creation and increase of abundance; these factors also lead to the inevitable breakdown of capitalism. At all three levels the idea of conflict is underscored: conflict between the ideal and reality, the moral issue; conflict between labor and capital, the sociological issue; conflict between growth and stagnation, the economic issue. Since this conflict generates change, capitalism, according to Marx, must eventually give way to another social system to replace conflicts and restore ethical, social, and economic harmony. This change is the "dialectical process" whereby socialism will replace capitalism. Thus, Marx created one of the world's most powerful ideologies, whose vision of abundance, equality, and freedom still stands as a challenge to classical-liberal individualism, to private property, and to private enterprise. In effect, it is a challenge to market democracy.[14]

NEOCLASSICAL CONTRIBUTIONS

The rise of socialism, the demand for social justice, and Marx's use of instruments of the dominant ideology to attack its legitimacy (e.g., the labor theory of value and the theory of capital accumulation) prompted a search for a theoretical defense of the existing system. In part, the new defense was that of the philosophy of the individual developed and cultivated by dominant business and economic interests from the mid-nineteenth century beyond World War II. In effect, it is a reinforced version of the laissez-faire argument discussed earlier in this chapter.

Economists did not take the extreme position of individualism very seriously. For one thing, Benthamite utilitarianism suggested that government intervention may be justified by the "greatest good" argument. For another, economists concerned themselves with pressing social issues for which the philosophy of extreme individualism provided little insight. This did not mean, however, that economists rejected the individual philosophy. On the contrary, they remained within its general framework.

More important, economists intentionally or otherwise developed a new theoretical apparatus that presumably served to refute the Marxian critique of capitalism. This was the neoclassical economics developed after 1870. In effect, the foundation of economics was reduced to the desires and wants of the individual, and the entire theoretical explanation of production, distribution, and prices was based on the single assumption of rational, individual self-interest. Neoclassical economics represented a significant scientific advance; it reduces to the simple but elegant idea of marginalism as a complex set of theories of value, distribution, and return to factors of production. The value of a product or service was seen not as the result of the amount of labor embodied in it, but as the result of the usefulness of the last unit purchased. With marginalism, a new approach to economics developed.

Carl Menger (1840–1921), William Stanley Jevons (1835–1882), Leon Walras (1837–1910), and Alfred Marshall (1842–1924) shifted the focus of economics from social classes and their economic interests (which had been underscored by David Ricardo and Karl Marx) to that of the individual.[15] The individual consumer became central to the theoretical apparatus of economics, which displaced the principle of income distribution envisioned by Ricardo as the mainspring of economic progress and the basis for Marx's theory of the breakdown of capitalism. The system of free markets does maximize individual welfare. Because consumers are assumed to maximize their satisfaction and because production responds to consumer wants, it follows that the result will be welfare maximizing. Moreover, marginalism also shows that the costs of production are pushed to the lowest level possible by competition. If allowed to operate without constraints, the entire economy becomes a pleasure-maximizing machine in which the difference between consumer benefits and production costs is increased to the highest level possible. In short, economics is transformed into a service consistent with the individualist social philosophy of Herbert Spencer and William Summer Graham.

The development served also to reinforce, at least in the United States, the legal theories of U.S. Supreme Court Justice Stephen Field (1816–1899) and the philosophy of unrestricted individualism in U.S. constitutional law. One result of Field's interpretation was the elimination of much state legislation dealing with economic affairs, including the regulation of hours of work, child labor, and factory condition. Private property was thus viewed as a natural right that no government could interfere with lightly.[16]

Marx's challenge was also taken up in the application of marginal analysis to income distribution, which demonstrated that all factors of production-labor and land-capital earn a wage exactly equal to their contribution to the value of output. Called the theory of marginal productivity, which is based on the last marginal unit, its conclusion is that workers would be paid a wage equal to the last unit of output they produced. The same idea was applied to profits earned from capital and to rent from land. In effect, to each factor of production the same law applied. No one could exploit anyone else because everyone received what he deserved. The entire product was exhausted, and no surplus value existed. Marx's concerns were simply irrelevant.

This happy state of affairs, critics are quick to point out, depends very much on the assumptions of the marginal productivity theory:

1. The theory rests on the assumption of perfect competition.

2. All factors of production must be completely substitutable for one another.

3. There must be no change in costs of production per unit of output as the level of production falls or rises. Not all economists are satisfied by such assumptions. Indeed, some economists have never accepted the theory of marginal productivity, which they view as singularly unreal.

It is the issue of periodic booms and depressions plaguing the rapidly industrializing countries that has attracted considerable public and government attention. During the first half of the nineteenth century, little concern was shown by most economists—thanks to their acceptance of the general propositions of Say's Law of Markets, which states that (1) there should be no periodic economic breakdowns, and (2) the economy should continue to operate at uninterrupted high levels of output and employment. In Say's Law the demand is created by production, and in the aggregate the two can never get out of phase with one another. Economists interested in business cycles typically sought causes outside the framework of production and distribution.

For instance, Stanley Jevons (1835-1882) developed a quantitative relationship between sunspots and business fluctuations. He argued that these fluctuations were connected with variations in the weather patterns affecting all of the earth, probably arising from increased waves of heat received from the sun at ten-year intervals. This simply serves to reinforce Say's Law, because the cause is outside the system of production and distribution. Perhaps the best interpretation within Say's Law is provided by the argument that the monetary system generates instability while the basic system of production and distribution remains stable. If the monetary and financial system is stable, general economic stability is assured.

In 1873 Walter Bagehot (in his now classic treatise on money and finance, *Lombard Street*) spelled out how it was to be done: Limit the expansion of credit to legitimate needs of business through effective action by the "central bank." This would prevent excessive credit issue from overstimulating the economy and thereby developing into a crisis. Once the situation got out of hand, the central bank could probably moderate the crisis, but the economy would simply have to weather out the storm.[17]

These theoretical advances served to firmly entrench capitalism and to defend it from its critics. The basic analysis of classical economics was supplemented by (1) marginal utility, (2) marginal productivity, and (3) the monetary theory of business cycles. The free-enterprise economy was pictured as operating to produce what consumers want, thus maximizing welfare by distributing products justly and by normally operating at full utilization of resources. The issue of laissez-faire in neoclassical economics was not a rigidly held doctrine. In fact, the major area of exception was monetary policy, which was assigned to the government and its agent, the central bank. It was their responsibility to preserve economic stability by properly managing the money supply to serve the legitimate needs of business. The Banking School influence in the form of the real bills doctrine is obvious here. Even so, such monetary intervention was to be held to a minimum and was to be strictly guided by the free market. In short, discretionary monetary policy was to be limited by the requirements of the free market and within the constraints imposed upon it by the gold standard. As a result, the scope was very limited for the exercise of discretionary authority by central banks.

Arguments raised in support of the mercantile, or banking school, tradition were based on two principal ideas:

1. The country's bank money will expand only in proportion to the needs of trade if banks restrict themselves to discounting only real bills of exchange; the converse will prevail when trade declines.

2. A country's currency will have a desirable elasticity only if commercial banks will maintain a reasonable liquid reserve position and will operate competitively.

The first idea, which stressed the limiting effect of quality on the quantity of loans, prevailed in the United States and elsewhere prior to 1860. Thereafter, the quest for elasticity and liquidity dominated the banking scene. These two concepts constitute what economists call the "real bills" doctrine.

Although the rationale of the real bills doctrine has been attacked throughout history by economists and others, it has never been completely vanquished. Indeed, the doctrine is firmly lodged in central and commercial banking practices. Supporters of the doctrine argue that it provides an intrinsic, self-regulating limit to the quantity of bank money. It provided the chief support for banking reform in the United States before 1913; the Federal Reserve Board embraced it thereafter. While the doctrine can be found in various qualitative control measures over bank credit, it also influences the preferences of central banks for interest rates and money market conditions as policy targets over monetary magnitudes.

Neoclassical economists also approved of other types of government intervention. Such intervention served to facilitate the operation of free competition and free markets. On this score, concern with monopolies and legislation designed to control their practices tend to be supported by most economists. The fact is that neoclassical economics does not adopt lock, stock, and barrel the simple individualism and laissez-faire policies, as critics assert; neither does it opt for wholesale intervention. It does accommodate the realistic needs of society. It does have strong ideological implications because it serves to rebuild the theory of free, private enterprise on a new basis, thereby making the refutation of Marx unnecessary. Private property and free private enterprise weathered the Marxist storm more or less intact, thanks to the efforts of neoclassical economists.

PHILOSOPHY OF THE WELFARE STATE

These issues, however, were not settled to the satisfaction of all concerned. At the close of the nineteenth century, a continuing concern about the complex nature of man and his society simply had not been adequately addressed—either by those who argued that society is the sum of individual units, brought into an easy equilibrium by market forces, or by those who argued that the social system is divided into antagonistic classes with social conflict fueling change. There was yet another view, one arguing that the chief objective of society is to promote human welfare; it was, in effect, the philosophy of the welfare state. Its exponents included such diverse entities as Roman popes, Fabian socialists, New Dealers, and Great Society advocates.

Papal economics attempted to come to terms with the social problems bubbling up from European industrialization and nationalism, which brought a new socioeconomic and political order to the continent during the last quarter of the nineteenth century. Pope Leo XIII (1810–1903) issued a series of encyclicals between 1871 and 1901 opting for the middle ground in the feud between labor and capital. The problem, argued Pope Leo, was not economic but moral. The solution must be based in justice animated by charity. Because these are nonmarket phenomena, they cannot be measured by the marketplace parameters of profit-loss and wages-costs.

The papal tilt was at first toward capitalism in the condemnation of socialism and the defense of private property. Subsequently, a compromise evolved in (1) an indictment of laissez-faire policies (*On Conditions of Labor*), (2) condemnation of socialism, and (3) support for private property rights and the natural rights of individuals. Harking back to theories of Thomas Aquinas in the thirteenth century, the papal appeal criticized the extreme individualism of the market economy and called for a return to human and community values.

Papal economics asserted that government intervention is justified whenever the welfare and preservation of society is threatened. In these matters, justice and fairness are to serve as guides. The tradition established by Pope Leo continued to influence later popes, Roman Catholic labor movements, and some political parties. The idea that man and community are one, along with emphasis on and reconciliation of both individual freedoms and individual welfare in a society that stresses community values and social justice, continues to be attractive.

For instance, Pope John Paul II's encyclical, written during the summer of 1981, was intended to be a sequel to the encyclicals of Pope Leo XIII (*Rerum Novarum*, 1891) and Pope Pius XI (*Quadragesimo Anno*, 1931).[18] Both are powerful social documents, and the new encyclical of John Paul II is a comprehensive statement on social issues. It backs labor unions, urges worker participation in management, and proposes a "just" family wage and subsidies that would free mothers from the necessity of taking jobs. The encyclical condemns both "rigid" capitalism and the "collectivist system" that eliminates all private ownership of the means of production. It suggests a socialist middle ground as a model for economic development. The central theme in the 99-page, 22,000-word encyclical (*Laborer Exercens—On human work*) opposes the "dehumanizing excesses" of modern economic systems.

The encyclical, written in Polish, reflects John Paul's vision of "a just society based on an ideal economic system." John Paul strongly endorses the workers' right to organize unions, to participate to some extent in the management of their companies, and to strike, except for political purposes or in essential public services. Radical and urgent changes are necessary to rescue farmers from the big landowners and "to restore to agriculture their just value as the basis for a healthy economy." Multinational corporations are engaged in the condemnable practice of fixing high prices for their products while trying to keep down prices for raw materials and semi-manufactured goods, thereby widening the gap between rich and poor nations. "In order to achieve social justice in various parts of the world, there is a need for new movements of solidarity of the workers and with the workers," according to Pope John Paul. It is sure to be studied carefully in the Soviet Union, in the Pope's native Poland, and in Latin America, as well as in other countries there the Roman Catholic church is influential.[19]

While the papists grappled with the social, economic, and political chaos in Europe brought about by an industrial society, Fabian socialists John A. Hobson and Richard H. Tawney in England promoted ideas and programs to deal with similar concerns. Essentially interventionist, their ideas cast government's role as one that assists man in developing his talents to the utmost. This was to be done by government working to remove barriers in man's path to the "good life."

A cascade of social legislation descended upon England as a result. Legislation dealing with factory safety became law in 1891 and 1895; limiting working hours for women and children in 1891; slum clearance in 1890; increased powers for labor unions in 1890–1900; workmen's compensation and child welfare in 1906; old-age pensions in 1908; town planning and redevelopment in 1909; sickness and disability insurance in 1911. In effect, while serving as mainstays to contemporary economies, many articles of welfare legislation were put into place by the turn of the century.

Even though their vision is behind much English social legislation, generators and spokesmen of unorthodox ideas such as John Hobson received little gratitude from significant numbers of their contemporaries. In fact, Hobson could not find employment in English universities. However, his writings—*Work and Wealth Incentives in the New Industrial Order, Physiology of Industry*, and *Evaluation of Modern Capitalism and Imperialism*—fortunately did much better.[20] Indeed, V. I. Lenin (1870–1924) incorporated into communist ideology Hobson's *Imperialism*, which attacked the selfish expansion of European states.

Like Hobson, Fabian socialists envisioned a society with the highest moral standards through a democratic socialist regime designed to promote as much happiness as possible, for the largest possible number. A small but influential intellectual group included such members as George Bernard Shaw, Sidney and Beatrice Webb, H. G. Wells, and Annie Besant. Named after the Roman general Fabius Maximus, "the delayed," who fought Hannibal with guerrilla tactics instead of frontal confrontation, the name signifies the society's philosophy and plan of action. Their vehicle, *Fabian Essays*, established in 1889 under the editorial leadership of Shaw, promoted gradual extension of state intervention in economic affairs to improve working conditions, to replace monopoly with government ownership, and to promote a more egalitarian distribution of income.[21]

Unlike the Marxists, the Fabians did not view the state as an instrument of class warfare that must be destroyed; rather, it was seen as a means of social control that, once seized, could be used to promote social welfare. They pushed successfully for the formation of a labor party with a socialist platform in 1906. Their tactics, in effect, involved political action within the framework of democratic, parliamentary government. In short, resort to persuasion rather than revolution was a singular Fabian characteristic. That these efforts bore fruit is indicated by the existence of the British Labor party and much of contemporary social and welfare legislation in Great Britain.

Drawing on world experience, the economic historian Richard Tawney (1880–1963) argued for a society reformed along the functional lines of a socialist society. Rewards are to be received by those productive members of society who expend work and effort in the tasks society requires, not to such unproductive elements as the promoter, speculator, and rentier who collect large sums of unearned income. Property rights, according to Tawney in *The Acquisition Society* (1920), should not be maintained if no service is performed. In *Religion and the Rise of Capitalism* (1926), he debated the issue raised by Werner Sombart and Max Weber over whether the Protestant Reformation created the intellectual atmosphere that made possible the rise of modern capitalism. He argued that the two are related, but also that modern society and its business activities are completely amoral. In *Equality* (1931), Tawney's theme is that egalitarianism can support and sustain a democratic political framework. In effect, it is through socialism that human values can receive their necessary development.[22]

The American approach to these same problems of industrialism is characteristically pragmatic, lacking much of the socialist philosophy prevailing in Great Britain and Europe. Workable solutions to specific problems are sought within the traditional framework of American society. Much of the necessary work is attributed to a small group of economists investigating such issues as business cycles, labor relations, monopoly, big business, and social welfare. Through their influence on progressive political leaders at the turn of the century and, later, the New Deal, the theme was promoted that modern industrial society faced serious problems that would not solve themselves. Government intervention was necessary if the destructive forces of the free market were not to have singularly tragic results for both society and the individual.

Thorstein Veblen (1857–1929) represents one of the more important economists through his influence on American reform thought. Essentially, his argument is that the fundamental forces of change are at work to require adaptations of the social, economic, and political institutions inevitably opposed by the establishment and represented by wealth and influence. He sees conflict between change and vested interests. His critique of the "pecuniary society" and the "business system" gave both direction and viewpoint to the movement for economic and social reform. Veblen's two books, *The Theory of the Leisure Class* (1899) and *The Theory of Business Enterprise* (1904), are considered economics classes.[23]

John R. Commons (1862–1945) and his followers formulated specific reform measures and legislation that were adopted first by some states and later incorporated into the New Deal platform of F. D. Roosevelt. Programs and policies such as utility regulation, collective bargaining, and mediation to settle disputes between labor and management on a voluntary basis, along with unemployment insurance and worker's compensation, promotion of economic growth, employment, and stability, are cases in point—clearly a remarkable achievement.

According to Commons, the government must serve as a mediator between conflicting economic interests and between economic forces and the individual. He does not necessarily reject the view of neoclassical economists that harmony emerges out of the equilibrating forces of the market, nor does he reject the Marxist view of class conflict. In fact, he goes beyond both of them to argue that the market can reconcile some but not all of the conflicting interests that arise in a modern economy. Continual conflicts emerge in such an economy, requiring government intervention to obtain equitable solutions.[24]

The New Deal philosophy in essence owes much to Veblen, Commons, and their followers. Through government intervention, the public is protected from the worst consequences of an industrial, market-oriented society. The philosophy represents a singular shift from the view of a harmonious, self-regulating, free-enterprise, market-oriented economy, as advocated by the classical and neoclassical economists.

The New Deal administration's intervention into the economy followed three paths:

1. Use of the federal budget to promote adequate aggregate spending in the economy to offset shortfalls in the private sector of the economy. It recognized government responsibility for economic stability in the economy. This recognition is now embodied in the Employment Act of 1946 and is institutionalized in the Council of Economic Advisors to the president.

2. Attempts to promote cooperation between businessmen and labor in various industries.

3. Government intervention into regional land-use planning based on water resources (e.g., the Tennessee Valley Authority).

According to the liberal reform philosophy of the New Deal (and in contrast to classical and to present-day liberal views), the individual does not necessarily contribute most to society by pursuing his own interest, nor is he necessarily responsible for all of his misfortune. Therefore, society must accept responsibility for the welfare of each individual to enable him to function effectively in society. The passage of welfare measures such as unemployment insurance, workman's compensation, social security, and federal grants-in-aid in health and education are aimed at providing security for the individual.

In addition, businessmen are to accept social responsibility beyond mere profit-making. The pre–New Deal situation whereby businessmen ran roughshod over human and social values is no longer tolerated. In short, business must justify itself by something more than profit. What that "something" is, however, is not specified. All of this does not serve to endear the reform liberals to the business community.

The liberal reform philosophy of the New Deal extended into President Truman's Fair Deal and, afterwards, into the short-lived administration of President Kennedy. It was picked up in the Great Society programs of President Johnson and was essentially carried on through the administrations of Presidents Eisenhower,

Nixon, Ford, and Carter. What appears to be a resurgence of neoliberalism and neoclassical economics through "supply-side" economics in President Reagan's administration has received considerable attention in the 1980s. The fact is that reform liberalism, as manifested in the past several U.S. presidential administrations, managed to restructure much of the country's economic and social framework without gross violations of individualism, private property rights, and the market-oriented private enterprise economy.

Events took a less satisfactory course in Russia and in Eastern European countries during and after the two world wars. War, revolution, and counterrevolution served to wreck what appeared to be promising liberal reforms, which began at the turn of the century and continued, although at a halting pace, into World War I.

At the time, Russia was the most backward country in Europe, with a primitive system of agriculture and an industry staffed by an illiterate population. By professing its allegiance to a Marxist ideology, which postulated that socialism would naturally evolve into highly industrialized economies for the working-class majority, Russia was at odds with received socialist doctrine. The country simply did not square with what Karl Marx and his followers had in mind. To complicate matters, the world revolution had failed, and the new Soviet state was surrounded by antagonistic capitalist countries who considered it an "illegitimate child of history."

V. I. Lenin (1870–1924) led the Bolshevik Revolution to a successful conclusion. He did so after convincing his followers that Russia could bypass the capitalist industrial era and move directly from an agricultural, semi-feudal society into an era of socialism. Lenin formulated the basic ideas on how to accomplish the goal of a socialist society, which meant that the large-scale industrialization of Russia would be the vehicle to build a working-class society to nurture socialism. This required an alliance between workers and peasants under a workers' dictator-ship, although priority was given to the construction of an urban and industrial society; however, Lenin died before his strategy was translated into specific programs of action. A debate on goals and means continued in the 1920s and 1930s until Joseph Stalin ended discussion with the first of the purge trials that were to shake the very foundations of the new Soviet state.

Stalin (1879–1953) manipulated the great urbanization-industrialization debate to his favor. The moderates—led by the leading Marxist theoretician, Nikolai Bukharin—argued for balanced economic development and postponement of world revolution until the Soviet state was strong enough domestically to support such a revolution successfully. Although urbanization and industrialization were to be encouraged, it was dangerous for the Soviet state to push the peasants too far and to threaten their loyalty to the regime any further. In short, a slower development pace tuned to the realistic possibilities of the Soviet state was prudent. Stalin called this approach the "right deviation."

Opposing the moderates was the so-called left wing of the Communist party led by Leon Trotsky (1879–1940), who, in fact, was Lenin's key man during the Bolshevik Revolution. The idea promoted by the left wing called for mobilizing the country's economy to the utmost, squeezing living standards in order to free resources for industrial development, and using the power of materials and export. According to their view, agriculture was to be collectivized and mechanized. In effect, the economy was to be deliberately unbalanced in order to force industrialization. As for the international scene, the Soviet state would never be secure in a capitalist world. As a result, it could best protect itself by exporting world revolution principally by demonstrating the superior productivity of socialism through economic growth.

At first, Stalin took the position of supporting rapid industrialization and forced draft development advocated by the left wing, but he ruled against collectivization of agriculture to avoid alienating the peasants. As for world revolution, he sided with the moderates and Bukharin to form an alliance, which drove Trotsky into exile. Thereupon Stalin sided with the left and opted for collectivization of agriculture, a rapid rate for the accumulation of capital beyond anything called for by Trotsky and his faction. This move also gained Stalin the support necessary to purge Bukharin. In essence, the debate resolved itself into the establishment of ambitious development goals and a planning apparatus to carry them out, with the Stalin dictatorship as the driving force behind it.

This became the modified Soviet model, which was imposed in Eastern European countries following World War II. It is also the model and system dropped by Josip Broz Tito (1892–1980) in Yugoslavia following the Tito-Stalin split in 1948. With Yugoslavia's escape to pursue its own, independent road to socialism through its unique model of "worker self-management," a new chapter in socialism began; the world would never be the same. The collapse of various socialist countries in the 1990s and subsequent reforms are testimony that the road is indeed a dead end.

With post–World War I Europe and the Bolshevik Revolution as background, one can gain useful insight into the efforts by John Maynard Keynes (1883–1946) to formulate new policies designed to preserve and revitalize the market economies of Europe. To Keynes, the challenge was clear enough. The Marxist-Leninist socialists had engineered a revolution that not only brushed aside everything before it but transformed a backward, rural economy into an industrial giant. Already weakened by war, European civilization was by now threatened with extinction.[25]

At the time, against apparent socialist success, Britain continued its deflationary policy designed to achieve international stability at the expense of internal stability, as it had in the post-Napoleonic years. Keynes argued that Britain's return to the gold standard at the British pound's prewar par would diminish British exports and would cause domestic wages, prices, employment, and output to fall. Keynes argued for a managed monetary system to replace the classic gold standard. His advice was disregarded, and Britain returned to the gold standard—only to realize the validity of his prophecy. Already crippled by war, the dissolution of its empire, and economic stagnation, Britain joined the rest of Europe to wait for a miracle. In Keynes's view, Europe could not afford to wait.[26]

This was Keynes's vision, although he lacked the theoretical apparatus to convince an audience educated in classical and neoclassical economics. To demonstrate the futility of the British government's deflationary monetary policy, he had to show the inadequacy of the classical theoretical apparatus, which rested on the relationship among the gold standard, the domestic level of employment, and Say's Law of Markets. Keynes realized the need to demonstrate convincingly the relationship between the theory of employment and monetary theory. He devoted more than a decade to the task.

The two-volume *Treatise on Money*, published in 1930, was Keynes's first effort to unravel the problem. Essentially, he argued the distinction between investment and savings and their different underlying motivations. Unlike Say's Law, which holds that the two must be equal, Keynes argued that this need not be the case. For instance, if savings are greater than investment, general economic activity will decline. Conversely, Keynes's policy prescription, which he argues in the various *Essays in Persuasion*, is similar in the *Treatise*: The monetary system should be managed to assist in maintaining equality between savings and investment in order to promote economic stability. In addition, a program of public works should be put in place to reduce the undesirable effects of economic depression on employment.[27]

The collapse of the world economy and the onset of the Great Depression of the 1930s created a political and economic environment that was receptive to the new ideas advanced by Keynes and others. Contributions to economics made by members of the National Bureau of Research, the University of Stockholm (the Swedish School)—including such economists as Knut Wicksell (1851–1926), D. H. Robertson, William T. Foster, W. Catchings, and others—paved the way for acceptance of Keynes's ideas, now presented in his *General Theory of Employment, Interest, and Money* (1936). The principles are essentially those he put forward in the *Treatise*. The new development in *General Theory* is the concept of equilibrium at less than full employment. Accordingly, an equilibrium is possible at a depression level; however, unless a change takes place in the relevant variables, the economy will stagnate indefinitely. These ideas stood in direct opposition to the classical and neoclassical theories dominating economic thought and practice for more than a hundred years.

For practical politicians in search of theoretical justifications for deficit financing already under way in many industrial countries, the *General Theory* came at the right time.[28] It provided a theoretical foundation to the commonsense view that large government expenditures financed by borrowing were needed to ease the hardships of the depression on the population. It appeared to recognize the advantages of a self-adjusting market mechanism, which was argued so eloquently by classical and neoclassical economists, although its important assumption that wages and prices are determined externally to the system was at odds with received theory. This was important, for it reinforced the theory's basic interventionist position. It called for government to manage the general level of economic activity in the interests of society in a manner consistent with individual freedom and a stable social order. In effect, Keynesian economics provides and articulates the theoretical framework for the reform-liberal policies promoted in the United States, Great Britain, and elsewhere since the beginning of the twentieth century. Keynes thus manages to give coherence to his vision and to socioeconomic and political changes accelerated by the tragedies of World War I and the collapse of the world economy in the postwar years.

Correct or not, Keynes offers a politically attractive alternative to received theories and policies, which appeared to be detached from reality. This does not mean that other explanations are not consistent with the evidence. I have discussed these explanations elsewhere and will again call attention to a number of them in later chapters of this study.[29]

NOTES

1. In the mountain of literature on the evolution of ideas, see Ellis T. Powell, *The Evolution of the Money Market, 1385–1915* (London: Frank Cass, 1966); Warren J. Samuels, "Adam Smith and the Economy as a System of Power," *Review of Social Economy* (October 1973), pp. 123–37; L. Rogin, *The Meaning and Validity of Economic Theory* (New York: Harper & Row, 1958); J. J. Spengler and W. R. Allen, *Essays in Economic Thought* (Chicago: Rand McNally, 1960); George Stigler, *Production and Distribution Theories* (New York: Macmillan, 1941); J. Dorfman, *The Economic Mind in American Civilization*, Vol. 3 (New York: Viking Press, 1949); E. K. Hunt, *History of Economic Thought: A Critical Perspective* (Belmont, Calif.: Wadsworth, 1979); Carl Menger, *Problems of Economics and Sociology* (Urbana: University of Illinois, 1963); J. A. Schumpeter, *History of Economic Analysis* (New York: Oxford University Press, 1954); Ludwig von Mises, *The Anti-Capitalistic Mentality* (New York: D. Van Nostrand, 1956); E. J. Hamilton, A. Rees, and H. G. Johnson, eds., *Landmarks in Political Economy*, selections from the *Journal of Political Economy* (Chicago: University of Chicago, 1962); Frank H. Knight, *The Ethics of Competition* (New York: Augustus M. Kelley, 1950); E. Whittaker, *Schools and Streams of Economic Thought* (Chicago: Rand McNally, 1961); J. Viner, *Studies in the Theory of International Trade* (New York: Harper and Bros., 1937); D. Vickers, *Studies in the Theory of Money* (Philadelphia: Chilton Co., 1959).

2. In some of the early writers, we see anticipations of theories advanced much later. See, for example, Thomas Joplin (1790–1847); Thomas Attwood (1783–1856); Nicholas Barbor (1640–1698); William Lowndes (1652–1724); Bishop George Berkeley (1658–1783); John Locke (1632–1704); Richard Cantillon (1697–1734), *Essai sur la nature du commerce en général 1730–1734*; and John Law (1671–1729), *Money and Trade Consider'd with a Proposal for Supplying the Nation with Money* (1705, 2d ed. 1720). D. Vickers, *Studies in the Theory of Money, 1690–1776* (Philadelphia: Chilton Co., 1959), makes the point that there was more Keynesian-type economics in the early period than has often been recognized.

3. See David Hume (1671–1729), "Of Interest; Of Money" in *Essays, Moral, Political, and Literary*, Vol. 1 of *Essays and Treatises* (Edinburgh: Bell and Bradfute, Cadell, and Davis, 1804).

4. For example, Anna J. Schwartz, *A Century of British Market Interest Rates 1874–1975* (London: The City University, 1981), writes that Henry Thornton (1760–1815), who in his *Enquiry into the Nature and Effects of the Paper Credit of Great Britain* (1802) expressed concern about the British monetary system during the Napoleonic era, understood

the fallacy of the real-bills doctrine; the distinction between the first round and ultimate effects of monetary change; the lag in effect of monetary change; the problem market participants faced in distinguishing relative from general price changes; the distinction between internal and external gold drains; the factors influencing the foreign exchanges including the role of purchasing power parity; how to bring inflation under control; the relation of the Bank of England to other English banks; types of effects of monetary disturbances on interest rates; the distinction between the market rate and the natural rate of interest and between nominal and real rates of interest. (p. 1)

See also the interesting exchange between Jacob A. Frankel and Charles R. Nelson in their article, "On Money," on whether David Hume believed in a stable long-run Phillips Curve: Charles R. Nelson, "Adjustment Lags versus Information Lags: A Test of Alternative Explanations of the Phillips Curve Phenomenon," *Journal of Money, Credit, and Banking* (February 1981), pp. 1–11; Jacob A. Frankel, "Adjustment Lags versus Information Lags: A 'Comment' and 'Reply' by Charles R. Nelson," *Journal of Money, Credit, and Banking* (November 1981), pp. 490–96.

   5. See Walter Bagehot (1826–1877) in his classic on money and finance, *Lombard Street* (1873).

   6. See J. J. Spengler, *Origins of Economic Thought and Justice* (Carbondale and Edwardsville: Southern Illinois University, 1980) for a useful review of the early contributions of economic thought as well as a bibliography.

   7. Adam Smith, *The Wealth of Nations* (1776).

   8. Thomas R. Malthus, *Definitions on Political Economy Preceded by the Rules Which Ought to Guide Political Economists in the Definition and Use of the Terms with Remarks on the Deviation from These Rules in Their Writings* (1827), and *Essay on the Principle of Population as It Affects the Future Improvement of Society* (1798).

   9. David Ricardo (1772–1832), *The High Rise of Bullion: A Proof of the Depreciation of Bank Notes* (1810).

   10. Jean Baptiste Say (1767–1832), *Treatise on Political Economy* (1803).

   11. Jeremy Bentham (1748–1832) in his classical works on political reform, democratic government, and majority rule.

   12. George Tavalas, "Some Initial Formulations of the Monetary Growth-Rate Rule," *History of Political Economy* (Winter 1977), pp. 525–47, writes: "Even more significantly, early formulations of Friedman's rule span backward to the writings of Jeremy Bentham [1748–1832] and Henry Thornton [1750–1815] at the start of the nineteenth century and to the neglected writings of John Gray, during the 1830s and 1840s" (p. 536).

13. Robert Owen (1771–1858), whose reform efforts included attempts to establish cooperative communities with land owned in common and worker-owned enterprises.

14. Karl Marx (1818–1883), *Das Kapital* (1948, originally published in 1867–1895).

15. Carl Menger (1840–1921); William Stanley Jevons (1835–1882); Leon Walras (1837–1910); and Alfred Marshall (1842–1924), *Principles of Economics* (London: Macmillan, 1930).

16. Stephen Field (1816–1899), United States Supreme Court Justice.

17. Walter Bagehot, *Lombard Street* (1873).

18. Pope Leo XIII (1810–1903), *Rerum Novarum (On Conditions of Labor,* 1891), which was the Magna Carta of labor; and Pope Pius XI, *Quadragesimo Anno* (1931).

19. Pope John Paul II, *Laborem Exercens (On Human Work, 1981).*

20. John Hobson (1858–1940), *Work and Wealth Incentives in the New Industrial Order* (1921); *Physiology of Industry* (1956); and *Evolution of Modern Capitalism and Imperialism* (1926).

21. G. B. Shaw, ed., *Fabian Essays* (1889).

22. Richard Tawney (1880–1963), *Acquisition Society* (1920); *Religion and the Rise of Capitalism* (1926); and *Equality* (1931).

23. Thorstein Veblen (1857–1929) wrote two economics classics: *The Theory of the Leisure Class* (1899) and *The Theory of Business Enterprise* (1904).

24. John R. Commons (1862–1945), *The Economics of Collective Action* (New York: Macmillan, 1950).

25. John Maynard Keynes (1883–1946), *General Theory of Employment, Interest, and Money* (New York: Harcourt, Brace, and Company, 1936); and *Treatise on Money* (1930).

26. It is useful here to quote John M. Keynes, "A Short View of Russia," *Essays in Persuasion* (New York: Harcourt, Brace, 1932):

On the economic side I cannot perceive that Russian Communism has made any contribution to our economic problems of intellectual interest or scientific value. I do not think that it contains, or is likely to contain, any piece of useful economic technique which we could not apply, if we chose, with equal or greater success in a society which retained all the marks, I will not say of nineteenth century individualistic capitalism, but of British bourgeois ideals. Theoretically, at least, I do not believe that there is any economic improvement for which Revolution is a necessary instrument. On the other hand, we have everything to lose by the methods of violent change.

In Western industrial conditions, the tactics of the Red Revolution would throw the whole population into a pit of poverty and death.

But as a religion, what are its forces? Perhaps they are considerable. The exultation of the common man is a dogma which has caught the multitude before now. *Any* religion and the bond which unites co-religionists have power against the egotistic atomism of the irreligious.

The modern capitalism is absolutely irreligious, without internal union, without much public spirit, often, though not always, a mere congeries of possessors and pursuers. Such a system has to be immensely, not merely moderately, successful to survive. In the nineteenth century it was in a certain sense idealistic; at any rate, it was a united and self-confident system. It was not only immensely successful, but held out hopes of a continuing crescendo of prospective success. Today it is only moderately successful. If irreligious Capitalism is ultimately to defeat religious Communism, it is not enough that it should be economically more efficient-it must be many times as efficient. (pp. 306–7)

27. John Maynard Keynes, *Treatise on Money* (1930).

28. See also the interesting discussion in W. R. Allen, "Irving Fisher, FDR, and the Great Depression," *History of Political Economy* (Winter 1977), pp. 560–87. John Kenneth Galbraith writes, in "Came the Revolution" (Review of Keynes's *General Theory*), *New York Times Book Review* (May 16, 1965):

By common, if not yet quite universal agreement, the Keynesian revolution was one of the great modern accomplishments in social design. It brought Marxism in the advanced countries to a halt. It led to a level of economic performance that now inspires bitter-end conservationists to panegyrics of unexampled banality. For a long while, to be known as an active Keynesian was to invite the wrath of those who equate social advance with subversion. Those concerned developed a habit of reticence. As a furtive consequence, the history of the revolution is, perhaps, the worst-told story of our era. (p. 34)

Useful on this score are sections of the four essays published by *The Economist* to commemorate the century of J. M. Keynes's birth: Milton Friedman, "A Monetarist Reflects," *The Economist* (June 4, 1983), pp. 17–19; F.A. Hayek, "The Austrian Critique," *The Economist* (June 11, 1983), pp. 39–41; Paul Samuelson, "Sympathy from the Other Cambridge," *The Economist* (June 25, 1983), pp. 19–21; John Hicks, "A Skeptical Follower," *The Economist* (June 18, 1983), pp. 17–19.

29. See George Macesich, *The International Monetary Economy and the Third World* (New York: Praeger, 1981), Chap. 2; George Macesich, *The Politics of Monetarism: Its Historical and Institutional Development* (Totowa, N.J.: Rowman and Allanheld, 1984).

3

The Key Role of Money

A STABLE MONETARY ARRANGEMENT

If reform is to be successful, the key role that money plays in society must be explicitly addressed. Our discussion suggests the importance that writers in the classical and neoclassical traditions have attached to money. Its importance is underscored in the reform processes because it comes between man and his objectives. Some writers, including nineteenth-century Marxists who regarded the idolatry of money as a species of reification, argued that it is alienating or an illusion for man to believe that he can possess through wealth what he has lost through work—his essence and being.

Thus it is that Georg Simmel, for example, identifies two likely sources of trouble for the human institution of money.[1] First, because individuals do not receive income in kind but in money, they are exposed to the uncertainties originating from fluctuations in the purchasing power of money. Second, the very success of a "free monetary order" encourages the development of socialist or collectivist ideas, which serve to undermine the individualistic order based on free markets and money.

Monetary uncertainty will tend to move the social order away from the use of money and markets toward a greater reliance on some form of greater government control or command organization, thereby strengthening bureaucracy and its political influence. Furthermore, monetary instability and market failure are closely linked and both serve to weaken the social fabric.

Use of the monetary system and monetary policy to pursue changing goals and objectives threatens society's responsibility to maintain trust and faith in money. This in turn casts doubt on the monetary organization and, indeed, on market democracy itself. The nineteenth-century view of society's responsibility to maintain trust and faith in money was supported by the bitter eighteenth-century experiences with currency excess. Most classical and neoclassical economists underscored society's responsibility to preserve trust and faith in money.

Many of these economists would be less than enthusiastic in support of discretionary monetary policy to exploit the presumed short-run non-neutrality of money in order to increase permanent employment and output by increasing the stock of money. They would agree that although an arbitrary increase in money will not necessarily disrupt relative prices permanently, such manipulation sets into motion forces whose consequences for social stability are very serious indeed. Because no human power can guarantee against possible misuse of the money-issuing authority, to give such authority to government is to invite destruction of the social order. For this reason, they argued, it is best to tie paper money to a metal value established by law or the economy.[2]

John Maynard Keynes, in *Economic Consequences of the Peace* (1919), told us there is no better means to overturn an existing social structure than to debauch the currency.[3] He also alleged that Lenin had espoused that the best way to overthrow the capitalist system was to debauch the currency. Ironically, some can argue that Keynes's subsequent teaching opened the floodgates of inflation in the post–World War II period, even though he personally attempted to close those gates shortly before his death in 1946.[4]

Keynes clearly shared a monetary heritage with the classical and neoclassical schools of economic thought. What sets him apart are his views on the conduct of monetary policy. For example, Milton Friedman writes that he disagrees with the views Keynes expressed in *A Tract on Monetary Reform* in terms of the appropriate method for achieving a stable price level. Keynes favored managed money and managed exchange rates, that is, discretionary control by monetary authorities.[5]

The exercise of discretionary policy by monetary authorities that Keynes advocated is the issue that underscores his differences with monetarists led by Milton Friedman and F. A. Hayek's Austrians. Setting aside the monetary role of gold as a barbarous relic places Keynes in disagreement with the Austrians. His desire to place the execution of monetary policy at the discretion of public-spirited and competent civil servants sets him in disagreement with monetarists who argue for a growth rate rule for some definition of the money supply.

The value of market democracy is questioned by people who do not believe that it is possible to make it work in terms of specific goals that, in their opinion, society should pursue. The exercise of market democracy implies that it is possible for individuals to choose between a multiplicity of ends. This in turn requires that no arbitrary or capricious steps be taken to alter this exercise in favor of particular individuals, groups, or interests. The importance of money and the monetary organization is clear. A stable and predictable monetary policy cannot survive if it is directed to the shifting goals of price stability, full employment, economic growth, and economic equality. It will change with the goals adopted.

GUIDELINES FOR MONEY IN REFORM

It is useful to consider briefly the guidelines put forward by important views of money for a stable monetary organization to serve reform. If monetarist guidelines are adopted, there must be acceptance of monetarism's principal tenet (i.e., the quantity theory of money) that inflation is at all times and at all places a monetary phenomenon. Its principal policy corollary is that only a slow and steady rate of increase in the money supply—one in line with the real growth of the economy—can ensure price stability.

Milton Friedman summarizes the monetarist view on the relationship between the money supply and price level.

1. There is a consistent, although not precise, relationship between the rate of growth of the quantity of money and the rate of growth of nominal income.

2. This relationship is not obvious to the naked eye—largely because it takes time for changes in monetary growth to affect income. How long this process will take is within itself a variable.

3. An average change in the rate of monetary growth produces a change in the rate of growth of nominal income about six to nine months later. This is an average; it does not hold in every individual case.

4. The changed rate of growth in nominal income typically shows up first in output and hardly at all in prices.

5. The average effect on prices comes six to nine months after the effect on income and output, so the total delay between a change in monetary growth and a change in the rate of inflation averages around twelve to eighteen months.

6. Even after allowances for delays in the effect of monetary growth, the relationship is far from perfect, for there are many slips twixt the monetary change and the income change.

7. Short-term monetary changes of five or ten years primarily affect output over decades, although the rate of monetary growth affects prices primarily.[6]

The monetarists' view, as summarized in Friedman's *Counter-Revolution*, questions the doctrine advanced by Keynes that variations in government spending, taxes, and the national debt could stabilize both the price level and the real economy. This doctrine has come to be called the "Keynesian Revolution."

The "Austrian School," through members such as Carl Menger, Georg Simmel (a sociologist), Ludwig von Mises, and Friedrich von Hayek, provides useful insights into the monetary system as an integral part of the social structure. These insights also serve as guides to monetary reform. The Austrian views differ significantly from both Keynesian and monetarist views, although Milton Friedman and some monetarists come closer to the Austrians in their emphasis on monetary rules and a stable monetary order.

According to the Austrian view, money and the monetary system are the unintended product of social evolution in much the same fashion as is the legal system.[7] Money is a social institution, a public good. It is not simply another durable good held in the form of "real balances" by utility-maximizing individuals or profit-maximizing firms, as Keynesian and monetarist views hold. However useful the tools of supply and demand analysis may be when applied to money as a private durable good, Keynesians and monetarists miss the full consequences of monetary instability.

In essence, the monetary system is an integral part of the social fabric whose threads include faith and trust, which makes possible the exercise of rational choice and the development of human freedom. This is misunderstood by the very people who benefit from it. It is this misunderstanding of the social role of money as a critical element in the market mechanism and the need for confidence in the stability of its purchasing power that came to dominate much of Keynesian and monetarist thought in the postwar period. This misunderstanding is the ideological key to the use of discretionary monetary policies for monetary expansion as an unfailing means of increasing output and employment and of reducing interest rates.

Herbert Frankel writes that Keynes, following Georg Friedrich Knapp, presents the monetary system as a creation of the state. As such, it is available for manipulation by government consisting mostly of wise and well-educated people who disinterestedly promote the best interests of society. The fact that such an arrangement curtails individual choice and decision did not disturb Keynes, who saw little reason to believe that choice and decision benefit society. In essence, it is at best an elitist view of government that was familiar to Great Britain at the turn of the century; at worst, it depicts a totalitarian government on the model of the Soviet Union.[8]

David Laidler takes exception to Frankel's argument that Keynes is the architect of short-run monetary policy that seeks to exploit monetary illusion. According to Frankel, this exploitation tricks people into taking actions that, if they could correctly foresee the consequences, they would not take. Such trickery was not the policy product of the 1930s, when Keynes believed that undertaking an activist monetary policy to deal with unemployment would be what individual agents desired (but were prevented from accomplishing on their own because of price and market mechanism failures). In effect, Keynes thought he was dealing with the issue of involuntary unemployment. It was during the 1950s and 1960s that the idea of a stable trade-off between inflation and unemployment generated a "money illusion" that was available for exploitation by policymakers.

In my view, Laidler is correct in that policies derived from the Keynesian philosophy of money may not be the fundamental reason why faith in the institutions of a free society is threatened. Nonetheless, the policies of the 1950s, 1960s, and 1970s do owe much to Keynes's followers, if not to Keynes himself. Keynes did provide the theoretical apparatus that made possible the articulation of his post–World War I vision. It was in the late 1970s and 1980s that the "chickens came home to roost," with the era of rational expectations and growing distrust of government.[9]

According to followers of the Austrian School, one can attribute too much responsibility to Keynes and his followers for the lack of faith and trust in the "old order." Indeed, the durability of the old order was questioned by Simmel long before Keynes and his followers appeared.

This durability is questioned by Simmel throughout his *Philosophy of Money*. As we have noted, he is concerned not simply with money as a unit of account—a store of value and medium of exchange—but with (1) the free-market economy of which the monetary system is an internal part, and (2) the relationship between the institution of this economy and justice, liberty, and the nature of man as a social being. The focus is on exchange as one of the most fundamental functions that ties individuals into a cohesive social group. Because barter exchange is inconvenient, there naturally developed (1) a group of individuals who are specialists in exchange, and (2) the institution of money, which solves the problem of the dual coincidence of barter. As soon as money enters the picture and the dual coincidence of barter is resolved, exchange ceases to be a simple relationship between two individuals. Simmel notes that the ensuing generalization of claims made possible by money-transfers places these claims for realization upon the general economic community and upon government as its representative.

Unlike other things that have a specific content from which they derive value, money derives its content, according to Simmel, from its value. In turn, its value owes much to the implicit guarantee given by society and the community; it owes little to the physical properties of money. In effect, its value is based on confidence in the sociopolitical organization and order. In this view, the British pound sterling and the U.S. dollar owe their value more to the political and economic power and prestige of their institutions than to the physical properties of the pound and the dollar. This confidence in the political and economic institutions of a country is "trust."

Trust, then, is the ingredient that bonds society together; the more of it individuals have in a society's institutions in general and in its money in particular, the more extensive and intense the use of money will be in an economy. By and large, the consequences of such developments are beneficial to society in that man's achievements are enhanced not only in the economy but in all other endeavors as well. Indeed, freedom and justice are promoted by the development and growth of exchange and the monetary economy.

Consequently, the individual is able to act independently of other individuals while at the same time becoming more dependent on society as a whole. That is, an individual becomes more dependent on the achievements of individuals and less so on the peculiarities of personalities. The loosening of bonds serves to promote economic freedom. It may or may not promote political freedom at the same time.

Keynes, too, was concerned with monetary stability, the fragile nature of a money-using market economy, and the social order that went with it. He was also well aware of the need for trust in the stability of purchasing power if the market mechanism was to function properly. Indeed, to Keynes money was not just another commodity. A money economy is very different from a barter economy. The idea was lost, according to David Laidler and Nickolas Rowe, as the Hicksian IS-LM (Investment/Saving–Liquidity/Money) interpretation of Keynes's *General Theory* came to dominate monetary economics. The dominance of this incomplete version of Keynes in subsequent debates has surely been the main reason for their participants having neglected the Austrian ideas on those matters.[10]

However, the story is very different on the conduct of monetary policy, in which Keynes and his followers depart significantly from the Austrian and monetarist paths. These differences are so profound that they overwhelm areas of agreement. As we have noted, Keynes believed firmly in discretionary monetary policy and viewed the gold standard as a relic. Modern Austrians hold to the gold standard. The monetarists argue for a given growth rate in the stock of money. The difference between the Austrians and the monetarists is essentially over the means to achieve agreed-upon ends, although the latter do not stress the role of stability in promoting trust and thereby facilitating the functioning of markets. The Austrians, while distrusting the bureaucrats, are more skeptical than monetarists about the stability of the demand for money function. Consequently, they argue for pegging the price of money in terms of gold, relying on the stability of the relative price of gold in terms of goods in general.

Frankel, in *Two Philosophies of Money*, directs attention to the erroneous "nominalist" theories of money that imply that money is something external to the fabric of society, a thing or commodity in its own right, which governments are entitled to manipulate in pursuit of their own limited economic or social ends. He compares the views of Simmel and Keynes, arguing that both understood the economic uses and psychological power of money. Simmel and Keynes were also sensitive to money's influence on human character and behavior. More important, perhaps, Frankel demonstrates how the views of Simmel and Keynes summarize the conflicting ideologies of the nineteenth and twentieth centuries and serve to place contemporary monetary problems in perspective.[11]

Differences in monetary views will manifest themselves in reform guidelines. Thus, Keynes and many of his followers believed that a free monetary order might not work in terms of specific goals that, in their opinion, society should pursue. This view leads to utopian attempts to make the uncertain certain by control of society according to plan as well as by transformation of man. Its adherents believe that we now possess the technical tools and scientific knowledge that enable us to control monetary behavior, not only within a nation, but even internationally, and thereby to control not only the rate of economic change, but progress also. Monetarists, on the other hand, would support Friedman's view that "we are in danger of asking it to accomplish tasks that it cannot achieve and, as a result, in danger of preventing it from making the contribution that it is capable of making."[12]

What guidelines for reform are forthcoming from Keynes? According to John R. Hicks, Keynes founded the labor standard and its dependence on society's sociopolitical processes when he searched for a workable monetary standard in *General Theory*.[13] Keynes's efforts were translated into a managed monetary standard and yielded readily to discretionary monetary manipulation by authorities. The consequent monetary uncertainty generated by such manipulation has had the effect of casting doubt on the credibility of these authorities, their policies, and ultimately on the monetary regime itself. In the process, the long-term price level has lost its anchor. These are only the more obvious unintended consequences of Keynes's efforts.

The unintended consequences of Keynes's search for a workable monetary standard are but another illustration of money in history and the unintended perverse effects of human actions and decisions. The best intentional changes do at times lead through unintended consequences to undesirable results. Keynes's efforts are no exception.

Indeed, the idea that unintended effects of human actions and decisions often have unforeseen consequences became popular during the eighteenth century. At about the same time, another idea confidently supported the belief that institutional changes can be engineered to bring about a perfect society.[14] The idea of the perfectibility of the social order arose primarily during the course of the French Enlightenment, while that of the unintended consequences was a principal contribution of the contemporary Scottish moralists.

The idea of a perfectible society is deeply embedded in critiques of social and economic order. By the beginning of the nineteenth century, the idea served to launch strong criticism of capitalism and the social and economic order it represented. In the twentieth century, the idea also served Keynes in his search for a workable monetary standard.

In fact, Keynes's flexibility and fine-tuning propensities are certainly consistent with ideas flowing from the French Enlightenment. His propensities, writes Friedman,

> were in accord with his elitist political philosophy, his conception of society run by an able corps of public spirited

intellectuals entitled to power that they could be counted on to exercise for the masses. They may also have been related to an excessive confidence in his ability to shape public opinion.15

Keynes's flexibility and attribution to others of his own capacity to change his views by changing circumstances also led to serious misreading of matters far removed from economic policy.16

An example of Keynes's flexibility and misreading of events is provided by Hayek when he writes, "I am convinced that he owed his extraordinary influence in this field [economics], to which he [Keynes] gave only a small part of his energy, to an almost unique combination of other gifts." He had gained the ear of the "advanced" numbers much earlier and had contributed greatly to a trend that was in conflict with his own classical liberal beginnings. In fact, in 1933 he had shocked many of his earlier admirers by publishing an essay, "National Self-Sufficiency," in the *New Statesman and Nation*. (The essay was reprinted with enthusiasm by the *Yale Review*, *Communist Science and Society*, and the *National Socialist*.)17

Hayek quotes Keynes from the essay in question:

> The decadent international but individualistic capitalism, in the hands of which we found ourselves after the war, is not a success. It is not intelligent, it is not beautiful, it is not just, it is not virtuous—and it does not deliver the goods. In short, we dislike it and are beginning to despise it.

Hayek writes that Keynes later (and in the same mood) stated in the preface to the German translation of *General Theory* that "he [Keynes] frankly recommended his policy proposal as being more easily adapted to the condition of a totalitarian state than those in which production is guided by free competition."18

Criticism of capitalism's shortcomings is a view that Keynes shared with other contemporaries. Of course, Keynes was a man with a very sharp sense of history, theory, and policy. In chapter

24, "Concluding Notes on the Social Philosophy towards which the General Theory Might Lead," of *General Theory* he wrote that "the authoritarian state systems of today seem to solve the problem of unemployment at the expense of efficiency and freedom. But it may be possible by a right analysis of the problem to cure the disease whilst preserving efficiency and freedom."[19]

Keynes, the liberal economist, was certainly well aware of the advantages of individualism and the capitalist market system. Thus, he wrote,

> the enlargement of the functions of government, involved in the task of adjusting to one another the propensity to consume and the inducement to invest, would seem . . . both the only practicable means of avoiding the destruction of existing economic forms in their entirety and the condition of the successful functioning of individual initiative.[20]

In effect, Keynes felt that shortcomings of the capitalist, market-oriented, individualist system could be overcome with appropriate policies of government intervention while at the same time preserving the system's efficiency and freedom. On this point Keynes was consistent with the eighteenth-century view that social engineering through appropriate government policies can improve society's lot. Indeed, Keynes was also consistent with the "self-destruction thesis" of capitalism discussed by Albert Hirschman (1982) and many other past and present writers, including conservatives and Marxists.

The serious misreading of public policy on Keynes's part suggested by Friedman and confirmed by postwar events underscores the importance of constraining a country's bureaucratic and political elite. It is clear that such constraint should occur within a system of well-defined rules, a point advanced by Milton Friedman and other monetarists. This is particularly the case in the application of monetary guidelines to reform.

The reason is straightforward. We do not have at our disposal scientific knowledge that would justify fine-tuning of monetary policy with any reasonable expectation of success. To give bureaucrats—in this instance, central bankers—discretionary power to fine-tune monetary policy is to ask them to do the impossible. Thus, monetarists (or quantity theorists) urge a policy system based on rules and nondiscretionary intervention in the economy. Its principal policy corollary, as we have noted, is that only a slow and steady rate of increase in the money supply—one in line with the real growth of the economy—can guarantee price stability.

This is, of course, disputed by people who prefer administrative discretionary intervention in order to maintain aggregate demand in the economy. The central issue in the disagreement, essentially, is over defined versus undefined, or discretionary, policy systems. On this score the major opponents of the monetarist position are modern Keynesians and central bankers. Their position is that defined policy systems are inferior to administrative discretion. In effect, the modern Keynesian position (and that of central bankers) does not involve a search for optimal decision rules for monetary (and fiscal) policy. Central bankers are more or less in accord; it is consistent with their view that the conduct of monetary policy is an "art" not to be encumbered by explicit policy rules.

The modern Keynesian approach is, in effect, the economic branch of the political interventionist position. Its defining principle is the extensive use of government power without definite guidelines or policy systems. It has important allies in central banks, with whom it shares many banking school ideas. Its opponents, including monetarists, are those who seek lawful policy systems and limitations on the undefined exercise of power by government.

John Culbertson puts it well:

A basic difficulty with undefined policy systems . . . is that since the policies to be followed are uncertain, they may prove to be disastrously inappropriate. Such policy systems are risky. The intellectual difficulty of the proponent of discretionary policy formation is a real one. If the policy matters, then certain correct choices must be made, which implies that power must reside in those particular men who will make the correct decisions—but in a context in which the correct choices themselves are asserted to be incapable of being defined (since it is the basis of rejection of defined policy systems). Inevitably, it seems, the approach implies the existence of an elite or priestly class that promises to accomplish the indefinable.[21]

For the discretionary outcome, it does matter which economist sits at the elbow of which president or prime minister after all. The monetarist position is that a political economist is really not needed, given a well-defined policy system.

The Austrian view of monetary guidelines includes some form of gold standard as constraint on the domestic and international monetary system. Gold proposals, however, have not met with notable success.[22] This is not surprising. What is often lacking in these proposals is an appreciation and understanding of the fact that the gold standard has been more than a monetary standard. It cannot be understood, as it cannot be operated successfully, except as part of the socioeconomic, political, and philosophical system in which it was developed. This system no longer exists, for reasons discussed previously.

Moreover, there is a tendency for some gold advocates to idealize the gold standard and to overlook some of its more troublesome aspects. Between 1815 and 1914 there were twelve major crises or panics in the United States—which pushed up interest rates, created severe unemployment, and suspended specie payments (conversion of the dollar into gold)—and fourteen minor recessions.[23] Between 1879 and 1965, a period when the United States was on some sort of gold standard (the dollar's final administration), the consumer price index rose by an average of only 1.4 percent a year. On the other hand, severe bouts of inflation were followed by periods of deep deflation in which prices actually fell. For example, during the 1921 world recession when production actually fell for only a few months, there were 30- to 40-percent cuts in manufacturing wages in some countries.

An alternative proposal, which was pushed from theory to practice by F. A. Hayek, is that governmental monopoly in the supply of money be abolished and that the provision of money be left to an unregulated market.[24] Hayek contends that with private provision of money, money users would receive a better product and the problems of business cycles would be ameliorated. Pre–1860 U.S. monetary experience with multiple private currencies, which Hayek's study examines, sheds light on the feasibility of such a proposal. The ultimate constraint on the U.S. monetary system was the specie, or gold standard; Hayek's proposal on this score is not clear.

Another reform proposal is to opt for a fiduciary monetary standard within a monetary constitution on the national level. This is essentially a monetarist proposal on the national level. It is suggested by Leland Yeager and James Buchanan, and it incorporates a Friedman-type rule on the rate of monetary growth.[25] On the international level, fully flexible exchange rates would replace the existing "dirty float" system of exchange rates.

One merit of these proposals for constraining the monetary system by a monetary constitution and rule is their implicit recognition that the nineteenth-century integration of market processes has been impaired over the past several decades by the emergence in every country of a greater measure of state intervention, and particularly by the discretionary nature of such intervention in the monetary sphere.

The monetarist measures advanced as guidelines for monetary reform are not necessarily a cure-all for troubles in the monetary system. They are in keeping with the objectives of those seeking defined guidelines within lawful policy systems. Because these measures could also constrain central bankers in their exercise of discretionary monetary authority and thereby limit the practice of their art, these measures are not likely to generate much enthusiasm—especially because central banks would become smaller and less influential bureaucratic institutions. Nonetheless, the uncertainty and the undesirable political implications of discretionary actions by government authorities, including central bankers, would be curbed.[26]

NOTES

1. Georg Simmel, *The Philosophy of Money*, trans. T. Bottomore and D. Frisby, with introduction by D. Frisby, (London and Boston: Routledge and Kegan Paul, 1977, 1978), p. 160.

2. Simmel, *Philosophy of Money*, p. 160.

3. John Maynard Keynes, *Economic Consequences of the Peace* (London: Macmillan, 1920).

4. F. A. Hayek, "The Keynes Centenary: The Austrian Critique," *The Economist* (June 11, 1983), p. 39.

5. Milton Friedman, "A Monetarist Reflects: The Keynes Centenary," *The Economist* (June 4, 1983), p. 19.

6. Milton Friedman, *The Counter-Revolution in Monetary Theory*, First Wincott Memorial Lecture (London: Institute of Economic Affairs, 1970).

7. David Laidler and Nickolas Rowe, "Georg Simmel's Philosophy of Money: A Review Article for Economists," *Journal of Economic Literature* (March 1980), pp. 97–105; S. Herbert Frankel, *Two Philosophies of Money: The Conflict of Trust and Authority* (New York: St. Martin's Press, 1977); review of Frankel's study by David Laidler in *Journal of Economic Literature* (June 1979), pp. 570–72.

8. For a discussion of this issue, see George Macesich, *The International Monetary Economy and the Third World* (New York: Praeger, 1981), chaps. 1–2 and references cited there.

9. George Macesich, *Monetary Policy and Rational Expectations* (New York: Praeger, 1987).

10. Laidler and Rowe, "Georg Simmel's Philosophy of Money," p. 103.

11. Frankel, *Two Philosophies*, pp. 4–6, 86–89, and 92–95.

12. Milton Friedman, "The Role of Monetary Policy," in *The Optimum Quantity of Money and Other Essays* (Chicago: Aldine Publishing, 1969), p. 99.

13. John R. Hicks, "The Keynes Centenary: A Skeptical Follower," *The Economist* (June 18, 1983), pp. 17–19.

14. See Albert Hirschman, "Rival Interpretations of Market Society: Civilizing, Destructive, or Feeble?" *Journal of Economic Literature* (December 1982), pp. 1463–84.

15. Friedman, "A Monetarist Reflects," p. 17.

16. Friedman, "A Monetarist Reflects," p. 18.

17. Hayek, "The Keynes Centenary," p. 41.

18. Hayek, "The Keynes Centenary," p. 41.

19. J. M. Keynes, *The General Theory of Employment, Interest, and Money* (New York: Harcourt, Brace, and World, First Harbinger Ed., 1964), p. 381.

20. Keynes, *General Theory*, p. 381.

21. John M. Culbertson, *Macroeconomic Theory and Stabilization Policy* (New York: McGraw-Hill, 1968), p. 535.

22. See a useful summary by M. D. Bordo, "The Classical Gold Standard: Some Lessons for Today," *Review*, Federal Reserve Bank of St. Louis (May 1981), pp. 1–16; R. M. Bleiberg and J. Grant, "For Real Money: The Dollar Should Be as Good as Gold," editorial commentary in *Barron's* (June 15, 1981); L. E. Lehrman and Henry S. Reuss, "Should the U.S. Return to the Gold Standard?" *Christian Science Monitor* (September 21, 1981). See *The Economist* (September 5, 1981), pp. 11–12, for the report of the U.S. Gold Commission studying a greater role for gold in the United States. See also Martin Bronfenbrenner, "The Currency-Choice Defense," *Challenge* (January/February 1980), pp. 31–36:

> The gold clause was relegalized by Section 463 of the U.S. code in October 1977. Little publicity has been accorded this change; few people know about it; any rush of gold clauses may lead Congress to reverse its 1977 action. On the other hand, that action may be a straw in the wind; it has friends in Congress; extension of the legal tender privilege to other currencies and thus freer competition between currencies may be closer in the U.S. market than anyone realizes. (p. 36)

See also Anna J. Schwartz, "The U.S. Gold Commission and the Resurgence of Interest in a Return to the Gold Standard," *Proceedings and Reports*, Vol. 17 (Tallahassee: Center for Yugoslav-American Studies, Research, and Exchanges, The Florida State University, 1983); Dr. Schwartz was executive director of the U.S. Gold Commission.

23. *The Economist* (September 19, 1981), pp. 17–18.

24. F. A. Hayek, *Denationalization of Money* (London: Institute of Economic Affairs, 1976).

25. See Leland B. Yaeger, ed., *In Search of a Monetary Constitution* (Cambridge, Mass.: Harvard University Press, 1962); James Buchanan, "Predictability: The Criterion of Monetary Constitutions," in Yaeger, *In Search*, pp., 155–83; Milton Friedman, "Should There Be an Independent Monetary Authority?" in Yaeger, *In Search*, pp. 219–43; Milton Friedman and Anna J. Schwartz, *Monetary History of the United States, 1867–1960* (Princeton: Princeton University Press for National Bureau of Economic Research, 1963); Milton Friedman, *A Program for Monetary Stability* (New York: Fordham University Press, 1959). See also Robert E. Lucas, Jr., "Rules, Discretion, and the Role of the Economic Advisor," in *Rational*

Expectations and Economic Policy, ed. S. Fischer (Chicago: University of Chicago Press, 1980), pp. 199–210; T. J. Sargent and N. Wallace, "Rational Expectations, the Optimal Monetary Instrument, and the Optimal Money Supply Rule," *Journal of Political Economy* 83 (1975), pp. 241–54.

26. A number of these issues are discussed in George Macesich, *The Politics of Monetarism: Its Historical and Institutional Development* (Totowa, N.J.: Rowman and Allanheld, 1984).

4

Constraints of Nationalism

THE ISSUE

Nationalism is one of the overriding passions of our time. Between 1945 and 1968, 66 new states were born out of the wreckage of old colonial empires. Each colonial struggle gave birth to new nationalisms and to the unity necessary to confront the external world of other states and to combat tendencies toward tribal or regional fragmentations within.

The nation-state model may have emerged historically as a Euro-American invention, but this form has been embraced worldwide. Market democracy, as typically practiced in liberal democratic states, is better equipped to deal with multinationalism than are its nondemocratic counterparts; and the more developed and entrenched market democracy is, the easier it is to arrive at a mutually agreeable solution.

Nationalism can take a number of forms. A narrow, militant, and rapacious variety has brought much grief and suffering to mankind.[1] Another is economic nationalism. This chapter focuses primarily on economic nationalism, whose exercise serves to severely constrain, if not undermine, market democracy.

THE CONCEPT OF NATIONALISM

Nationalism is derived from the word *nation* which itself had roots in the Latin *natio*, signifying birth. It had been taken to mean a social grouping with or without ties of blood. During the Middle Ages, the term *natio villae* was used to designate a kinship in the village. Later in the Middle Ages, students at the University of Paris were divided into nations according to their places of birth. Still later, the term *nation* was applied to the population of a country without regard for racial unity. By the late eighteenth century, *nation* began to be used abstractly and interchangeably with *country*.

Currently, scholars distinguish a nation from a race, a state, or a language. In particular, the emphasis is placed on a common political sentiment. The political term *nation* is used by some scholars to designate a people that "has attained state organization." For example, Hans Kohn places emphasis on "the political doctrine of sovereignty" as the principal characteristic of modern nations.[2] In effect, the contemporary connotation of nation is political.

The concept of nationalism is even less precise.[3] It can be taken to mean the historical process by which nationalities become political units in modern states constructed out of tribes and empires. It can be taken to mean the theory, principle, or ideal implicit in the actual historical process. It can be taken to mean the activity of a political party, thereby combining the historical process and political theory. It can be taken to mean a condition of mind among the members constituting a nationality, sharing commitment to the ideal of one's own national state or mission of the national state. It is, as Kohn suggests, "first and foremost a state of mind, an act of consciousness."[4]

Some scholars argue that the concept of nationalism is best understood by social psychologists. It is defined by some as the "self-consciousness" of a nation and by others as an "intolerant and aggressive instinct." Still others describe nationalism as a way of manifesting national spirit through (1) history, (2) traditions, (3) language, and (4) an abstract idea controlling the life and actions of a nation.

The characteristic of nationalism that many scholars agree on is that it reflects social mobilization whereby the commitment of an individual is transferred from the local to the national level.[5] In this view the individual becomes aware that his interests go beyond his local community to the national level. In effect, the individual turns from the local level to a national community for economic status, political loyalty, social dependence, cultural form, and psychological drive. Although it may differ from country to country, social mobilization in its various forms is the essence of nationalism.

In terms of economic policy, nationalism typically involves an ideological preference for a number of goals. These include as much self-sufficiency as possible; public ownership and public enterprise in key economic sectors; and intensive regulation and control of private, domestic, and foreign enterprise. In general, discrimination in favor of nationals is carried on as a matter of policy. This discrimination, however, is not uniform for nationals. There is a bias in favor of the ruling elite and the bureaucracy, which may be an investment in the creation and maintenance of a class deemed necessary for the construction and perpetuation of a viable national state for the common good.

There may be reasons other than economic nationalism why some governments pursue the policies just mentioned. For example, socialists are not necessarily nationals, yet they may prefer a collective economy for ideological reasons. Governments may also want external economics to be realized in pursuing protective trade measures on behalf of the industries of their nationals. The consequences, unfortunately, may be the same as those of pursuing parochial nationalist policies.

Nationalism continues to show vigor; the sense of national identity remains important. In confrontation with other "isms" such as capitalism, socialism, fascism, and communism, nationalism has been more resilient as a historical movement. In fact, many of the isms succeed only when they are identified with nationalism. Each nation, no matter what its size, is possessive of its sovereignty and does not intend to sacrifice even a small portion of its independence for the promised advantages of international cooperation. For such nations, nationalism of the Euro-American model is essential to ensure what they regard as freedom of decision and action. They prefer self-government with all of its dangers to servitude in tranquillity. They prefer to be governed by their own kind rather than by foreign administrators, no matter how efficient. The mental gymnastics required to justify nationalism in an interdependent world are all too evident.

Nationalist euphoria is inspired by economies that do not fulfill the hopes of their citizens. It is encouraged by the desire of the elite in many countries to attempt to insulate themselves from external differences and the dangers of votes, electoral or parliamentary, that express dissatisfaction with the course of economic affairs. The fact is that policies promoting economic nationalism as a means for promoting development have miscarried. As expected, they have served to cultivate and promote the interests and prosperity of the elite and the bureaucracy.

A competent and patient political leadership recognizes that nation-states that have given their citizens hope and rising living standards are more apt to become modern democratic states in the end. Indeed, the spirit of enterprise, independent judgment, desire for progress and change, knowledge of the world, and improved education are ingredients essential to these states. They are the very ingredients that are often lacking in a policy of economic nationalism.

Moreover, there are constraints as to what a country can do in its promotion of economic nationalism. These constraints are multidimensional; they include cultural, economic, monetary, and political elements. They are not simply internal to the country. More important, they are also external. Their net effects are to reduce a nationalist government's room to maneuver in promoting a policy of economic nationalism regardless of the skills and determination of its political leadership. What a country can do in today's interdependent world depends only in part on its size, location, resources, and the ethnic bases for its nationalism.

ECONOMIC IMPLICATIONS

The fundamental framework of this analysis draws its economic implications of nationalism from the works of Harry G. Johnson, Albert Breton, Anthony Downs, Gary S. Becker, and my own earlier work on economic policies in several countries.[6] It also benefits from conversations I had with Harry Johnson in the early 1960s on various topics dealing with the economics of nationalism.

Downs argues that political parties attempt to maximize gains from political office by catering to the tastes and preferences of voters. In a multiparty democratic society, political parties remain in office only by satisfying these tastes and preferences for various types and amounts of government programs. In effect, political power is exchanged for desired policies in a political transaction between party and electorate.

The critical element in Downs's hypothesis is the cost of acquiring information. He uses this cost to explain reliance on persuasion in arriving at (1) political decisions, (2) the inequality of political influence, (3) the role of ideology, (4) electoral apathy, and (5) the bias in democratic government toward serving producer rather than consumer interests.

Breton's analysis of economic nationalism identifies nationality with ownership by nationals of various types of property. It considers such nationality to be a type of collective consumption capital that yields an income of utility and that can be invested in by spending public funds in the acquisition of such capital. From these assumptions he derives a number of testable propositions about nationalism.

These propositions imply that nationalist policy is primarily concerned with redistributing, rather than increasing, income. The redistribution is from the working class to the middle class. As a result, there will be a tendency to resort to confiscation rather than purchase when the working class is poor. Since manufacturing jobs and ownership are preferred by the middle class, nationalism will tend to favor investment in national manufacturing. Given its collective nature, nationalism will strike a particularly responsive chord from socialists. Furthermore, the blossoming and appeal of nationalism will be closely associated with the rise of new middle classes who have difficulty in finding suitable career opportunities.

Johnson develops and extends Downs's cost of information regarding voter preferences; he extends the concept from Downs's established democracies to include emerging countries. Thus, the main obstacle to efficiency in the exchange between political parties and their electorate stems from ignorance on both sides about (1) prospective gains from policies offered and (2) the cost of acquiring the information necessary to make the exchange efficient. This obstacle forces the political party to depend on pressure groups, lobbyists, and communications media for its information about voter preferences. The dependence gives political parties a strong incentive to gain control over communications media in order to establish control over the country. Indeed, the recent push by emerging countries for a "new information order" is consistent with Johnson's hypothesis.

Given that the average voter is motivated by his own rational self-interest not to acquire much information about policies of political parties and the consequences for his economic welfare, whether well-informed or not he will have negligible influence on which party is elected. Here, ideology steps in to play a key role in political affairs. Ideology simplifies a political party's problem of communicating with its electorate. Its policies can be summarized in symbolism or slogans. Thus, the voter's problem is also simplified because he can vote by ideology instead of investing his time in evaluating each party's record and promises on a short range of particular policy issues. As a result, parties tend to compete through ideologies.

In established democracies, the type of party system depends on a variety of features, including (1) the distribution of ideological preferences among voters, (2) type of election system, whether by proportional representation or plurality, and (3) geographical distribution of voter preferences. Proportionality will tend to foster a multiplicity of ideologically differentiated parties. Plurality elections will tend to promote a two-party system, except where ideological differences are associated with geographical region. Actual policy in a multiparty system will tend to present a compromise among ideologies from the necessity of forming coalitions to obtain power. In two-party systems, the relation of party ideologies will be determined by the distribution of voter preferences for ideologies. Thus, if the distribution of voter preference for ideology is unimodal, there will be a grouping around a central ideological position and party ideologies will not differ significantly. On the other hand, if voter preferences are multimodal, then voter preferences that group around two or more ideological positions become very important. If a party departs too significantly from its ideological position, it may alienate its constituents, who will tend not to vote. Worse, if party ideologies are significantly different, the country itself will tend to be politically unstable and ripe for disintegration.

Matters are somewhat different when democracy is not well established. The incentive is for a political party to attempt to create a comprehensive and preclusive ideology to enable it to enjoy exclusive control of government. Emerging countries, observes Johnson, are particularly susceptible. In emerging countries this is reinforced because a change in government is likely to impose significant costs on those who have to wait for political office as opposed to those who hold power and political office permanently. To be sure, even in developed democracies the change of office by political parties tends to be wasteful. The economic and sociopolitical system in such countries tends to reabsorb ousted political office holders without imposing great private losses on them. Consequently, the ability of the economic and sociopolitical system not to impose undue losses on political losers, as well as the acceptance of the rules of the game of democracies and their principles, is important in cultivating workable democracies.

It is the nationalistic feeling that provides a foundation for the establishment of a preclusive ideology as a prerequisite for a single-party government. Johnson calls attention to the connection between the stridency of nationalism in emerging countries and their propensity to establish a one-party government. However, even where the two-party system is maintained, the competition in ideology would tend to make both parties stress nationalism and nationalist policies if there were widespread nationalist sentiment among the electorate. Johnson succinctly observes that only if there is a sharp division of voter preferences, with some voters envisaging serious disadvantages, would there be significant political division on the issues and the likelihood that political stability would be threatened.

Downs underscores that the working of political democracy will display a certain asymmetry between producer and consumer interests. The concentration will be on producer interests, often at the expense of consumer interests. Johnson extends this observation to nationalism and nationalist policies. Because producer costs can be spread thinly over a mass of consumers, nationalist policies win political support more readily by promoting producer interests even though the net benefits, taking consumers and producers together, tend to be negative.

Our theoretical framework outlines the workings of political democracy and party government, integrating nationalism in emerging countries into the framework. We can draw on Becker's work on racial discrimination and Johnson's interpretation to consider nationalism as a cultivated preference to call it a "taste for discrimination." That is, people who discriminate actually are willing to give up pecuniary returns for nonpecuniary or psychic income derived from avoiding the group discriminated against. In Becker's study the group discriminated against was Negroes in the United States. Johnson substitutes "taste for nationalism" for Becker's "taste for discrimination." Accordingly, the taste for nationalism attaches utility to certain jobs or certain property owned by members of the national group, even though pecuniary returns are forgone as a result of exercising such tastes.

The types of property and jobs to which such utility is attached are obviously the prestige jobs and socially significant property. For example, these include literary and cultural activities. Others include political and economic activities and properties with high prestige and incomes. The nationalist utility attached to the various properties, jobs, and cultural/other activities is derived internally from an emerging country's colonial era or externally by observing what takes place in more developed countries.

Nationalism is a collective consumption good or public good whereby its consumption by one individual does not exclude its consumption by others. The problem is one of determining the optimum amount of nationalism to supply. The specific benefits of nationalism obviously go to those select nationals who acquire offices or property rights in which nationalism invests. This would include the bureaucracy, elite, and producer interests. Thanks to the desire of cultural, linguistic, and communication interests to cultivate monopoly power, they are natural beneficiaries of a policy of economic nationalism. All of these interests are vulnerable to foreign competition.

Because everyone in the national state must consume the same quantity and quality of the public "nationalism" good, even though their preferences and tax payment for the good may vary, it is not surprising that there is considerable controversy on the output versus resource input of public goods by the nation-state. Some consumers want more and some less. Few will agree that the optimal quantity is truly optimal.[7]

As we have noted, collective decisions in political markets are complex. People can communicate their desires for public goods through voting behavior. Still, what a consumer-voter desires in a political market may be significantly different from what he or she ultimately receives. The correlation between a voter's choice and the expected outcome may be very weak. Efficient political decisions tend to affect everyone in the community, unlike decisions in a private market, which affect primarily the consumer and supplier of a given product or service.

Moreover, if the demand for nationalism as a "club good," to use James Buchanan's term, by the elite and the bureaucracy is added to the demand by the general population for a nationalism as a public good, it is likely that there will be an overproduction of nationalism. This will tend to allocate too many resources for the creation and preservation of the nation-state, including a formidable bureaucracy and military.

It is thus imperative that the bureaucracy and elite be discouraged and constrained from the use of nationalism to maximize their returns and advantages. One way is to structure the incentive system to prevent or limit the abuse of their authority. The method I recommend is a system of well-defined guidelines within lawful policy systems. In effect, I argue for a system of rules that constrains the bureaucracies and elites from the discretionary exercise of power. The more closely constrained the actions are by rules or performance criteria, the less will be their power and prestige and the less will their interests coalesce with promoting the excess production of nationalism.

As a public good, economic nationalism particularly appeals to the elite/bureaucracy and, perhaps, to specific producer interests, whereas the costs are spread out over the mass of consumers. Political support for nationalist economic policies is obtained on the basis of the gains they promise to their constituents, even if the total net benefits to all concerned tend to be negative.

As a policy, economic nationalism is encumbered by at least three biases.[8]

1. It concentrates on industrialization at the expense of agriculture. The objective here is to achieve a modern-looking nation-state as quickly as possible. The bias for industrialization is usually very specific on the types of industries to encourage. Selection is more on the criteria of what leading developed nations possess than on comparative advantage and economic logic. The establishment of a steel industry, an automobile industry, and a national airline are the more obvious examples.

2. It has a preference for economic planning. There is the feeling that controls associated with planning enable a country to more quickly mobilize available resources to achieve other desired goals of nationalism. Imitation of the Soviet Union's experience and its rapid postrevolutionary development into a world power recommends a course of national economic planning to some people. In general, there is the perception that the processes of economic development are speeded up by planning. Finally, the elite and the bureaucracy see planning as a direct means to exercise and enhance their power and prestige.

3. A policy of economic nationalism harbors indiscriminate hostility to large multinational or transnational corporations. They are viewed as agents of colonialism and imperialism for the advanced countries they happen to have their headquarters in and thus pose a threat to national sovereignty and independence. In effect, these corporations are viewed simply as an arm of the economic and political power of their parent countries. Because these corporations are more than likely independent entities, they are viewed with suspicion by both host and parent countries. The parent countries complain that such corporations ought to invest and produce more at home rather than sending employment opportunities abroad and creating balance-of-payments problems for the country.

It may be that nonpecuniary gains by the mass of the population from the collective consumption umbrella of nationalism offset losses in primary income imposed by economic nationalism policies, so that nationalist policies do result in maximizing total satisfaction. It may also be that nationalist policies are the simplest and cheapest means to raise real income in some emerging countries.[9] Indeed, economic nationalism may block economic growth to the extent that it becomes necessary to resort to even more extreme nationalist sentiment and policy as the only means for maintaining the illusion of economic development.

The economic significance of nationalism is to cultivate and extend property rights and jobs to nationals in order to satisfy their taste for nationalism. Confiscation and nationalization are but vehicles for this policy, which would include property and, very likely, jobs. Investment is another route whereby public funds are used to purchase property and create jobs and activities on behalf of nationals. It would also include imposing tariffs and protecting the activities of nationals, who would thereby receive higher prices that are, in essence, taxes imposed on the general consumer.

By reducing the efficiency of the country's economy, these by-products of economic nationalism will also reduce its real income. Disappointment with the economy's performance increasingly pushes the government into formation of prices and wages to ensure desired outcomes, which will typically lead to wage and price controls. Because wage and price controls inevitably fail, the system is increasingly driven into collective participatory planning where wages and prices are determined. In fact, this may be desired by some people. Nevertheless, this arrangement offers little chance that the market system will be allowed to play its effective and efficient role.

The inevitable failure of price and wage controls is readily demonstrated by problems and price results for individual products and services, including wages. The effects of a fixed price for a product or service depend on the level at which it is fixed and whether it is a minimum or maximum price.

To illustrate the issues, suppose we set up an administrative agency to fix prices. Now suppose this agency fixed the price of a commodity or service at a level whereby it would fall relative to other prices if there were no price controls and if the price were established by free-market forces. In this case, the price control will have no effect and our agency will have performed a needless exercise. Of course, the administrative costs incurred by this exercise will be borne by the taxpayer.

Now suppose that our agency sets a fixed price that is a maximum price, but it sets the price at a lower level than what the price would have been if determined by free-market forces. Then shortages will appear. People will want to buy more of the commodity or service than they otherwise would, but less of the product or service will be produced than ordinarily. Why should less of the product be produced at this lower price? The simple reason is that at this lower price it becomes more profitable to produce other items whose prices are not fixed at this lower level. Now, if more is demanded than is supplied, then some system determines who among the people is going to get the product or service in question. This can be done by attaching another office to our price-administering agency, whose function will be to issue coupons; or the product or service can be given to old and regular customers of the suppliers; or it can be done according to the rule of "first come, first served." This is, of course, the familiar case of the queue with attendant losses in time spent waiting one's turn.

If less of a product or service is produced because its price is fixed too low, it must be that fewer resources are employed. Now, what happened to those resources? They simply move to other industries that produce products and services whose prices are not controlled. Ironically, since prices that tend to be controlled in "essential" industries are not controlled in "nonessential" industries, this means that price controls tend to cause fewer of the essential products or services to be produced and more of the nonessential products or services.

What I have just described need not be the case at all, because the government can induce producers of the commodity or service in question to produce more at the lower price by offering them an incentive in the form of a subsidy. This means that producers now receive a higher price, which has been raised artificially by government subsidy. The taxpayer will now bear not only the cost of the price-administering agency but also the additional cost of the subsidy.

Consider our last case, in which a minimum price is fixed at a level higher than what would prevail in a free market. Now there will be initial surpluses. At the higher price for the product or service, more will be produced. Instead of rationing to the consumer, it will now be necessary to ration production of the product or service among the many producers who would be willing to produce at the higher price. Again, as in the case of consumers, this can be done by attaching an office to our price-administrating agency whose function will be to allocate the product or service in question by quota production.

In general, this is an all-too-familiar problem of past U.S. agricultural surpluses. In this case, the taxpayer as a consumer will very likely pay the higher price for the product or service as well as the cost of the administering agency.

Moreover, selective price controls cannot avoid discrimination. If a producer's selling price is fixed, there is usually an obligation to control his costs. This means fixing more than the prices of a producer's more obvious inputs such as labor and raw materials. It also means that items such as taxes, interest costs, and business costs must also be fixed.

Control of labor costs, however, is the most difficult. Elements of labor costs such as fringe benefits, compensation for overtime work, shift differentials, and paid leave serve to complicate the already difficult task of setting wage rates. The U.S. federal minimum wage example illustrates the difficulties in setting wage rates.[10]

The inverse relationship between changes in the minimum wage and substitution (capital for labor) effects one would expect from economic theory appears to be confirmed. When information on evasion and violations of the minimum wage law is taken into account, considerable light is shed on the complexities of wage fixing. In effect, an increase in the minimum wage is equivalent to a reduction in the price of evasion and avoidance. The price of evasion and avoidance is the cost of evasion and avoidance minus the benefits of evasion and avoidance. The benefit has increased with the increase in the minimum wage. Other things being equal, one would expect evasion and avoidance of the minimum wage to increase. This also appears to be confirmed by the evidence.[11]

The minimum wage has had adverse effects on wage differentials,[12] and these differentials serve a useful purpose in allocating labor services into various occupations. They are an essential part of the price mechanism. When they are subjected to an autonomous shock by government fiat, a compression of wage differentials occurs. The wages of those directly affected by the rise in the minimum wage rise more than the wages of those not so directly affected. Because it is not as easy to allocate labor services as it is to allocate other services and goods, the problem of production adjustments is aggravated.

Matters are further complicated by difficulties in defining exactly what it is that is being controlled. Failure to specify accurately the end product or service leads to the inevitable tendency to increase profit margins by cutting quality, particularly where shortages already exist. The problem is not simply one of quality deterioration; it includes the tendency to reduce the variety of products.

Because of domestic price and wage ceilings, there is always the tendency for a producer to sell abroad at a higher price. When the producer is allocated fewer productive resources than he desires, he may seek to increase his supply by imports. This inevitably leads to price controls and physical controls over imports, such as foreign exchange controls and import and export quotas. The general direction into which a country adopting such controls is pushed forces its government and bureaucracy into being the sole judge of the volume and direction new investment will take. Government and its bureaucracy dominate the field of new investment through policies on profits and sales.

Even more important, failure to allow the market system to play its effective and efficient role almost guarantees that money and the monetary system will not be allowed to play a nondiscriminatory and autonomous role within the constraints of a rules-based policy system, which is necessary to assure the preservation of economic and monetary stability in the country.

Worse still, the pursuit of economic nationalism in today's interdependent world is a threat to worldwide stability. For small and emerging nations, it is a prescription for disaster because they are most likely to be dependent on foreign trade and the good will of other nations. Promoting economic nationalism through various protective measures invites and encourages retaliation by others. These activities serve to undermine not only the stability of the nation-state promoting economic nationalism but world stability and prosperity as well.

NOTES

1. Useful discussions of nationalism in English are presented by Louis L. Snyder, *Varieties of Nationalism: A Comparative Study* (Hinsdale, Ill.: The Dryden Press, 1976); K. W. Deutch, *Nationalism and Social Communication: An Inquiry into the Foundations of Nationality* (New York: John Wiley, 1953); E. H. Carr, *Nationalism and After* (New York: Macmillan, 1945); S. W. Baron, *Modern Nationalism and Religion* (New York: Harper, 1947); L. W. Doob, *Patriotism and Nationalism: Their Psychological Foundations* (New Haven: Yale University Press, 1964); C. J. H. Hayes, *The Historical Evolution of Modern Nationalism* (New York: R. R. Smith, 1931); F. O. Hertz, *Nationality In History and Politics* (New York: Oxford University Press, 1944); H. Kohn, *The Idea of Nationalism* (New York: Macmillan, 1944); F. Znaniecki, *Modern Nationalities: A Sociological Study* (Urbana: University of Illinois Press, 1952); B. C. Shafer, *Faces of Nationalism* (New York: Harcourt Brace Jovanovich, 1972); Harry G. Johnson, ed., *Economic Nationalism in Old and New States* (Chicago: University of Chicago Press, 1967); K. E. Deutsch and W. J. Poltz, eds., *Nation-Building* (New York: Atherton, 1963); E. M. Earle, ed., *Nationalism and Internationalism: Essays Inscribed to Carlton J. A. Hayes* (New York: Columbia University Press, 1950); A. Eban, *The Tide of Nationalism* (New York: Horizon Press, 1959); H. A. Gibbons, *Nationalism and Internationalism* (New York: Stokes, 1930); G. P. Gooch, *Nationalism* (New York: Harcourt Brace and Howe, 1920); F. H. Hinsley, *Nationalism and the International System* (London: Hodder and Staughton, 1973); O. Jaszi, *The Dissolution of the Habsburg Monarchy* (Chicago: University of Chicago Press, 1929); L. L. Snyder, *The Dynamics of Nationalism* (Princeton, N.J.: Van Nostrand, 1964); George Macesich, *Economic Nationalism and Stability* (New York: Praeger, 1985).

2. Kohn, *The Idea of Nationalism* (New York: Macmillan, 1944), p. 20.

3. See Hayes, *The Historical Evolution of Modern Nationalism*.

4. Kohn, *The Idea of Nationalism*, p. 20.

5. Snyder, *Varieties of Nationalism*, defines nationalism as

that sentiment of a group or body of people living within a compact or noncontiguous territory, using a language or related dialects as a vehicle for common thoughts and feelings, holding a common religious belief, possessing common institutions, traditions and customs acquired and transmitted during the course of common history, venerating national heroes, and cherishing a common will for social homogeneity. (p. 25)

In any given situation one or more of these elements may be absent, as Snyder points out, without affecting the validity of the definition.

6. Harry G. Johnson, ed., *Economic Nationalism in Old and New States* (Chicago: University of Chicago Press, 1967); Albert Breton, "The Economics of Nationalism," *Journal of Political Economy* 72 (1964), 376-86; Anthony Downs, *An Economic Theory of Democracy* (New York: Harper, 1957); Gary S. Becker, *The Economics of Discrimination* (Chicago: University of Chicago Press, 1957); George Macesich, *Commercial Banking and Regional Development in the United States: 1950-60* (Tallahassee: Florida State University, 1963); George Macesich, *Yugoslavia: The Theory and Practice of Development Planning* (Charlottesville: University of Virginia, 1964); George Macesich, "The Theory of Economic Integration and the Experience of the Balkan and Danubian Countries before 1914," in *Proceedings of the First International Congress on Southeast European Studies*, Sofia, Bulgaria, 1966, and *The Florida State University Slavic Papers* (1967); George Macesich, "Economic Theory and the Austro-Hungarian Ausgleich of 1867," in *Der Österreichisch-ungarische ausgleich, 1867* (The Austro-Hungarian Ausgleich), ed. Ludovit Holitik (Bratislava: Slovak Academy, 1971); George Macesich, *Geldpolitik in einem gemeinsamen europäischen markt* (Money in a common-market setting) (Baden-Baden: Nomos Verlagsgesellschaft, 1972); George Macesich, "Supply and Demand for Money in Canada," in *Varieties of Monetary Experience*, ed. David Meiselman (Chicago: University of Chicago Press, 1971), pp. 249-96.

7. See James M. Buchanan, *The Demand and Supply of Public Goods* (Chicago: Rand McNally, 1968); James Buchanan and Gordon Tullock, *The Calculus of Consent* (Ann Arbor: University of Michigan, 1962); Fred R. Gladbe and Dwight R. Lee, *Microeconomics: Theory and Applications* (New York: Harcourt Brace Jovanovich, 1980); Ronald Coase, "The Problem of Social Cost," *Journal of Law and Economics* (October 1960), pp. 1-45.

8. See Harry G. Johnson, "Ideology of Economic Policy in New States," in Johnson, ed., *Economic Nationalism*, pp. 129-30.

9. See Johnson, ed., *Economic Nationalism*, p. 15.

10. See George Macesich and Charles T. Stewart, Jr., "Recent Department of Labor Studies of Minimum Wage Effects," *Southern Economic Journal* (April 1960); Marshall R. Colberg, "Minimum Wage Effects on Florida's Economic Development," *Journal of Law and Economics* (October 1960); John M. Peterson, "Recent Needs in Minimum Wage Theory," *Southern Economic Journal* (July 1962); Yale Brozen, "Minimum Wages and Household Workers," *Journal of Law and Economics* (October 1962);

and L. G. Reynolds, "Wages and Employment in the Labor-Surplus Economy," *American Economic Review* (March 1965).

11. Macesich and Stewart, "Recent Department of Labor Studies," p. 288.

12. George Macesich, "Are Wage Differentials Resilient? An Empirical Test," *Southern Economic Journal* (April 1961).

Bureaucracy and Market Democracy

FORCES INCREASING AUTHORITY

Our discussion suggests the extent to which the exercise of market democracy has been modified by interventionist ideas. Certainly, experience with the Industrial Revolution and its upheaval and later events had much to do with the promotion of these ideas from theory to practice.

One consequence of the practice of interventionist ideas was increased authority of the state and its bureaucratic apparatus. This expansion was expedient but inglorious, necessary but dangerous, useful but costly. Along with the expansion came growing concern over the ability of the public to deal on equal terms with the maximizing behavior of an "artful and ever active" bureaucracy and political elite. Experience confirms that constraints must be placed on the exercise of discretionary authority by vote-maximizing bureaucrats and political elites if market democracy is to thrive and prosper.[1]

The public must insist that such constraints be put in place. Indeed, it was that shrewd observer of American democracy, Alexis de Tocqueville, who warned in the first half of the nineteenth century that democracy could falter as a consequence of citizens' diminished interest in restraining central authority.[2] He noted that because democratic man would not be able to count on his neighbors for support, he had an incentive to increase the power of the central authority.

Even earlier, the American founders—for instance, James Madison—were aware that their project, the federal constitution, was an exercise in constructing government out of defective human parts. They believed that the urge to tyrannize others was so strong that external restraints became absolutely indispensable. The image of man in their discourse appears less than free and rational because his will and intelligence may be at the service of his "passions," forces beyond himself that make self-control improbable. In both the Federalist and anti-Federalist political factions, a vague egalitarianism also led to the fear of elitism— "the artful and now active aristocracy" usurping the power that belonged to an unalert and passive people, as Walter Lippmann succinctly put it when he informed Americans that the framers of the Constitution had bequeathed to future generations of Americans a government of checks and balances.

As we discussed earlier, the task of constraining the bureaucracy and political elite is made all the more difficult by utopian attempts to make the uncertain certain by control of society according to plan. Our illustration of monetary policy, albeit important, is but a case in point. Monetary uncertainty originating primarily from fluctuations in the purchasing power of money will tend to move the social order away from the use of money and markets toward a greater reliance on some form of greater government control or command organization, thereby strengthening bureaucracy and its political influence. Moreover, monetary instability and market failure are closely linked and both serve to weaken the social fabric.

Another illustration, which will serve bureaucracy, is the rise of socialism in the 1930s, which promoted central economic planning and the redistribution of income policies. The Keynesian Revolution stressed the failure of the economic system, which was avoidable by the application of scientific knowledge. Harry

Johnson is surely correct when he writes that these two movements reinforced one another.[3] In turn, this led to the view that economic backwardness can be traced to defects in the private enterprise system and market democracy, not to the backwardness of people and their cultures in relation to the requirements of modern industrial society. Since the 1960s, the Third World has promoted this view to the top of the world's development agenda through demands for a new international economic order (NIEO).[4]

THE STATE AND BUREAUCRACY

Rapid sociopolitical and economic change, particularly since the Great Depression, has brought with it a growing bureaucratic influence as well as increased demands for reform to constrain bureaucracy's taste for discretionary authority. This urgency is underscored by growing evidence from the experience of former socialist countries of Eastern Europe. The violations of public trust and confidence by domestic bureaucracies in those countries are now common knowledge.

The fact is, however, that a government and its bureaucracy do not operate in a vacuum. They are products of previous and present values and beliefs about what government should do and how it should be done. Modern bureaucracy is the result of cumulative theory and practice. Unlike the case of the former socialist countries, institutional change in general tends to be cumulative. Much of what we have and do today reflects lingering influences from the past. This is as true of countries undergoing the processes of reform as it is of more stable countries. The result is that the processes of reform are made ever more difficult and complex. Reformers must take into account that old ideas and vested interests never die but withdraw into enclaves, small and large, where their partisans prepare for and await the moment of return. Many interventionist ideas, as we have discussed, promoted more active government involvement and responsibility for the (1) conditions of the economy, (2) level of unemployment, (3) stability of prices, (4) advance of productivity, (5) rate of growth, (6) inequity and injustices in the distribution of revenue, (7) condition of the environment, and (8) quality of life. These are expectations and responsibilities that only a very powerful government and its bureaucracy could meet. Government and its bureaucracy grew and expanded to meet these challenges.[5] Such expansion is certainly more than the liberal state envisioned. This is in contrast to a world of private societies where individuals are free to engage and disengage in trade or any other form of social intercourse and where the supreme social value is liberty.

In its theoretical ideal, market democracy is a minimal state. That is, individual interests are overriding. Happiness, satisfaction, and fulfillment must be sought for and can only be obtained by the individual in his or her own way, by reference to his or her own preferences, needs, and potentiality. The social well-being is simply the sum of individual satisfaction, and the social purpose is no more than the sum of individual purposes. Thus, market democracy cast on a liberal state has no purpose and no value other than to facilitate and protect the individual pursuit of personal values and private ends. In this view the state is subordinate to, and intended only to protect the security and property of, the individual. For this purpose it lays down and enforces rules for the exercise of property power, lest the freedom of one transgress upon the freedom of another. It must draw boundaries on the rights of property, lest the claims of one trespass on the prerogatives of another, resulting in endless conflicts between ownership and ownership, between claim and claim. It must provide for the interpretation and enforcement of contracts entered into voluntarily by private parties in the process of exchanges.

Clearly, market democracy as a limited liberal state is primarily juridical.[6] It can do without an extensive and powerful bureaucracy. It cannot, however, do without a strong judiciary. It is a limited bureaucracy consisting primarily of judges, juries, prosecutors and defenders, advocates representing interests before the bar, and police who enforce the rulings of the courts.[7] It is essential to the operation of the market economy. The single skill appropriate to the bureaucrat is that of the lawyer.

By way of illustration, consider the American experience. The American state is basically juridical in character, and until the Great Depression it was also a limited liberal state.[8] By constitutional fiat, as well as in practice, the American state did not have

> the autonomous power to intervene, control, plan, direct or in any way significantly affect the cause of internal events, or the structure of relationships, or the distribution of wealth and incomes, or the output of industry, or the character of like, or the nature of the economy.[9]

According to this view, bureaucracy as such is singularly constrained in a strict support position to the freely acting, self-interested profit seeker.

The catastrophic collapse of the trading world during the period between the two world wars cast into doubt the viability of an essentially liberal state with its essentially juridical function. The Keynesian Revolution insisted that the economic system is not self-equilibrating and self-adjusting. Keynesians argued that the interwar economic collapse can be attributed to self-perpetuating insufficiency of aggregate expenditure. Hence, aggregate expenditure must be controlled and held at the level where labor would be fully employed. Only the state, in their view, has the power and responsibility to manage aggregate expenditures.

There is nothing new in the position that the state must bear responsibility for doing what the free market left undone. As we discussed earlier, classical liberalism in the nineteenth century, with its strong bias against state intervention, nonetheless came to perform a host of functions—albeit to service the local needs the market did not satisfy.[10] What is new is that the sovereign power of the state is called upon by the Keynesian Revolution to manage an essential dimension of the entire economic system. The state must now stand responsible for the general level of employment of the country's human and physical resources. The juridical and defense functions of the lawyer and soldier in the limited juridical state are now expanded to include the economist, whose prime task is to manage the country's aggregate spending. This joining of the new professional competence of the economist, the lawyer, and the soldier called forth an expanded state bureaucracy.

By way of contrast, the Marxist perception of the state and its bureaucracy has long remained a critique of capitalism without reference to the deep and both unresolved and resolved problems of every socialist regime. These include (1) the reconciliation of the individual with collective values, (2) the organization of creative change, (3) the recruitment and selection of leadership, (4) the transference and control of power, and (5) the development of effective planning and rationale for collective choice.[11]

To be sure, the classical Marxist conception of the state and its bureaucracy is that it serves to usher in and assure a classless communist society; once achieved, it would wither away. Following the Great Depression and World War II, Western capitalism did not follow Marxist predictions even though organized labor gained and maintained political control of the state and its bureaucracy. Neither private property nor the capitalist mode of production changed as a result of political control by labor. As we have discussed, growing intervention in the economy served to constrain laissez-faire liberalism and the operation of the market economy. The consequent emergence of the welfare state, which curbed capitalism and guaranteed the development of industrial trade unionism, transformed the state of the "dominated" classes. The net result has been to change the Marxist conception of the capitalist state as well.

The neo-Marxist theory of the state now views the capitalist state as functioning with the legitimacy of its authority based on universal suffrage. Thus, it does have the consent of the governed and the cooperation of the dominated, as well as dominating, classes. This is reinforced in part through income transfers and welfare guarantees that serve to satisfy the universal needs of all functional groups. The support is further buttressed through an apparatus of acculturation, socialization, and education that instills ideologies of individualism and nationalism, and through the juridical system that emphasizes values and focuses on private property rights and prerogatives. The net effect is to encourage the development of values stressing individualism rather than collective, group, or class values. The theory thus does not abandon the idea of the state as an instrument of class or the importance of the bureaucracy as its instrument.

Still another perception of bureaucracy is that of the nationalist state. A strict nationalist state typically finds its meaning in war or threat of war. It develops its strength, organizes all of its resources, directs and controls the energies for its people in a perpetual readiness for, preparation for, or engagement in war. It is a maximal state and usually a military state as well. Its bureaucracy is well positioned to carry out the mandates of a nationalist state; and, as we have discussed, the bureaucracy also pushes nationalism for its purposes.

Thus, the nationalist state puts forth the idea of people who are one and indissoluble, who are bound together instinctively, who recognize their differences from all other people, and who are filled with a national spirit that gives to each a pride, a significance, and a meaning. In effect, one people, one bond, one law, one coin, one sovereign—and a bureaucracy to carry out its interests.

Nationalism represents a collective consumption good or public good whereby its consumption by one individual does not exclude its consumption by others.[12] The specific benefits of nationalism obviously go to those select nationals who acquire offices or property rights in which nationalism invests. This would include the bureaucracy, the elite, and producer interests. Thanks to the desire on the part of cultural, linguistic, and communication interests to cultivate monopoly power, they are natural beneficiaries of a policy of nationalism, especially of its economic dimension.

If the demand for nationalism as a club good by the elite and the bureaucracy is added to the demand by the general population for nationalism as a public good, it is likely that there will be an overproduction of nationalism. This will tend to allocate too many resources for the creation and preservation of the nation-state, including a formidable bureaucracy and military. It is thus imperative that the bureaucracy and elite be discouraged and, indeed, constrained from the use of nationalism to maximize their returns and advantages.

The growing role of government was not arrested in the postwar period but, indeed, was accelerated as a consequence of superpower tensions over basic political issues that quickly gained worldwide dimensions. In such an environment new governments with a liberal orientation did not relinquish complete control of resources for production, research, and development to the civilian sector and the free market. Given the nature of the military and space demands for scientific input, it is unlikely that the civilian sector would have been able to meet these demands in any case.

These circumstances served to reinforce Keynesian ideas of managing aggregate expenditures by (1) encouraging/discouraging private investment through central bank manipulation of money supply and interest rates and (2) judicious budgeting of surplus/deficit at the source of public spending. The justification can be found in the Great Depression, which occurred as a consequence of a downward shift in aggregate spending (producing mass unemployment) because prices did not move freely. Prices neither registered scarcities nor equilibrated available resources to output preferences. Contrary to the neoclassical theory of prices, the evidence suggests (according to the Keynesian view) that prices were administered and controlled in modern industrial economies. Large corporations, unions, and other bureaucratic organizations—not a multitude of self-seeking individuals in competitive interaction—set prices. These organizations have the marketplace in which to set and administer prices. They are not answerable to a wider public, but only to their own constituencies. As a result, prices become a function of autonomous and arbitrary power that is neither answerable for its effects nor responsible for its consequences to society at large.

Efforts to monitor and control the exercise of arbitrary power on the part of these organizations increasingly pushes the government into the formation of prices and wages to ensure desired outcomes. This will typically lead to an increased role for the state bureaucracy to administer wage and price controls. Because wage and price controls inevitably fail, the system is increasingly driven into collective participatory planning where wages and prices are determined—and, as we have discussed, this may, in fact, be desired by some people. Nevertheless, such an arrangement offers little chance that the market system, rather than a bureaucracy, will be allowed to play its effective and efficient role.

The net effects are an ever-increasing role and power for the state's bureaucracy, erosion of the market mechanism, and demoralization of its participants. How can such a growing power be monitored and harnessed, or held accountable, or have its parameter fixed; or how could the electorate participate in the formulations of its policies? One way, of course, is for the state to undertake increasing supervision. However, this merely exacerbates the problem and follows the only too familiar sequence of having the state undertake more control and more complex responsibilities. In this sequence the issue for the individual ceases to be the liberty to choose and decide; rather, it becomes that of accepting whatever is decided upon by the state and the bureaucracy.

Such activity by the state and its bureaucracy is no longer peripheral to and supportive of the operation of the competitive, price-directed market. Indeed, it casts aside the conception at the heart of neoclassical economics of a universe of individual self-seekers in competitive interaction, with resources and preferences optimally equilibrated by a free-moving price, mobilizing and locating scarce goods and services. In its place comes the view of a world of large organizations, having enormous power to administer and control price as a function of organizational policy, and being neither answerable nor responsible to anyone other than those within the organization itself.

The exercise of autonomous and arbitrary power has also made useless much of the Keynesian prescription that was offered as a cure for capitalism's ills. The supportive manipulation of the money supply, interest rates, and aggregate spending in order to remove unemployment is absorbed by higher wages and higher prices, raised at their own initiative to benefit large organizations. This leaves unsolved the problem of general and specific unemployment. The state is left as the only agency capable of confronting the exercise of such power. As a most likely result, its own power would be increased at the additional expense of individual decisionmakers.

Perceptive scholars have long called attention to the emergence of a new class, which they have called bureaucratic and managerial. Neither capitalists nor workers were really running things. On the basis of expertise, a new group had insinuated itself into power everywhere. The enormity and complexity of the tasks facing contemporary society have served to promote the interests of this group.

These issues prompt scholars to increasingly devote their talents to determining what must be done to overhaul and direct the state and its bureaucracy to more effectively serve the desires and interests of its electorate. Intelligent and rational constraints must be designed against the exercise of arbitrary power by the state, its bureaucracy, and large autonomous organizations. It is counterproductive to heap abuse, contempt, and new tasks upon these bureaucracies without having a clear idea of what are and ought to be the rules for their behavior.

In another study, I have turned to cooperation theory, the theory of public choice, and economics for helpful insights into bureaucratic and political behavior.[13] According to public choice theory, politicians and bureaucrats are just like other people: They are driven chiefly by egocentricity, not by altruism. For example, the theory teaches that because politicians respond to pressure groups and the desire to be re-elected, the actions of government will often create or magnify market imperfections rather than overcome them. Thus, proponents of the theory tend to argue that the actions of government should be limited. Accordingly, public choice theorists advocate (1) a constitutional amendment to require a balanced budget, (2) deregulation, and (3) as recommended in this study, a system of well-defined guides within a lawful policy system of rules to constrain the exercise of preference by the monetary authority for discretionary monetary policy.

Not everyone, of course, is prepared to accept the implications of the economic model for the behavior of the bureaucracy and the political elite. In particular, many are unprepared to accept the constraints on discretionary decisionmaking by the bureaucracy. They argue that impediments such as distinguishing facts from values, the ambiguous nature of goals, and the pressures and costs of information equation cast doubt on constraining the exercise of discretionary authority. In any case, some argue, goals cannot and should not be agreed upon in advance of decisions.

Moreover, critics note that political and economic choices are often conceived in different terms and are directed toward fulfilling different kinds of objectives; therefore, they should be evaluated by different criteria. For example, Aaron Wildavsky suggests that in a political setting a bureaucracy's need for political support assumes central importance, and that political costs and benefits of decisions are crucial. These costs and benefits, however, are very difficult to measure and quantify. Political benefits that might accrue to a bureaucracy may be evident enough: for instance, obtaining short-term policy rewards and gaining enhanced power over future decisions. Political costs might be less obvious and, according to Wildavsky, might need explicit categorization.

On this score he suggests "exchange costs," which are incurred when bureaucracies or political elites need the support of other groups or people.[14] "Hostility costs" may be incurred when, for example, a politician antagonizes some people and may suffer their retaliation. These hostility costs may mount and become "election costs," which in turn may become "policy costs" through his inability to command the necessary formal powers to accomplish desired policy objectives. Wildavksy also suggests "reputation costs," which arise from the loss of esteem and effectiveness with other participants in the political system and the loss of ability to secure policies other than those under immediate review.[15]

It is also possible, as we have seen, that bureaucracies tend to behave for political reasons, as suggested by Anthony Downs.[16] He describes a group of decisionmakers as "conservers" whose cautious behavior, minimizing individual or institutional risks, is inherently political. Motives of self-interest, which Downs assigns to "climbers" as well as to "conservers," are themselves political. "Mixed" motives of self-interest and altruism are also partly political. Only the primarily altruistic "statesman" seems to have the general good, not politics, in view. But, as Downs suggests, because the statesman does not compete for organizational resources, his function will simply be underfunded.

Most decisions, however they are measured, have political implications. The choice of criteria by which to measure decisional outcomes has political significance because of the possibility that adherence to a particular set of criteria will ultimately favor the political interests of one group over others. Indeed, caution must be exercised to avoid (1) the unthinking application of economic criteria to the measurement of political phenomena or (2) the assumption that economic rationality is, by definition, superior to political rationality.

Advocates of political rationality defend it on these grounds: (1) One can accept propositions that politics are legitimately concerned with enabling the decisional processes of government to function adequately, (2) basing decisions on political grounds is as valid as basing them on other grounds, and (3) rationality according to the currency of politics is as defensible as rationality in economic terms. Properly conceived and applied, political rationality can be a useful means for gaining insight into bureaucratic processes.

Traditional conceptions of bureaucracy and its role in government are not altogether accurate. These conceptions are, nevertheless, important in shaping views of bureaucracy. They include political neutrality in carrying out decisions of other government organizations; legislative intent as a principal guiding force for the actions of bureaucracy; legislative oversight of bureaucracy as a legitimate corollary to legislative intent; and direction by the chief executive—which, under separation of powers, creates the possibility of conflict over control of bureaucracy.

In the United States, moreover, significant problems arise from the fragmented nature of the various policy-making processes.[17] The U.S. bureaucracy functions in a political environment where there is no central control over policy; as a result, considerable slack in the system allows the bureaucracy considerable discretion. Moreover, not all decision-making power or authority is clearly allocated; this results in many small conflicts over fragments of power. The net result is that bureaucrats in the United States are often active in political roles and take policy initiatives that are not neutral, thereby departing from traditional views about bureaucratic roles and functions. They are, in effect, in a position to develop semi-independence from elected leaders. Their activity, furthermore, is organized around jurisdiction over particular policy areas (e.g., the Federal Reserve Board, monetary policy, and banking). They make a special effort to prevent changes in jurisdiction that might affect their political interests or those of their supporters (e.g., the Federal Reserve Board and its relations with federal and local authorities who deal with monetary and banking affairs).

Bureaucratic power and accountability are major issues in contemporary society. Bureaucratic power is based in good measure on the ability (1) to build, retain, and mobilize political support for a given agency and its programs and (2) to make use of expertise in a particular field (e.g., monetary and banking affairs by the Federal Reserve Board). Bureaucratic accountability, especially in the United States, is difficult to enforce consistently and effectively because of frequently conflicting interests in the legislative and executive branches of government. The issue of accountability is made all the more difficult by the fact that U.S. bureaucracies operate under authority delegated by both the chief executive and the legislative branch, and with considerable discretion to make independent choices (again, consider the Federal Reserve Board and its relations with Congress and the executive branches of government).

NOTES

1. See Milton Friedman and Rose Friedman, *Free to Choose* (New York: Avon Books, 1981) and Milton Friedman and Rose Friedman, *Tyranny of the Status Quo* (Orlando, Fla.: Harcourt, Brace, Jovanovich, 1984). See also George Macesich, *Money and Democracy* (New York: Praeger, 1990) and the studies and evidence cited there.

2. Alexis de Tocqueville, *Democracy in America* (Garden City, N.Y.: Doubleday, 1969).

3. Harry Johnson, "The Ideology of Economic Policy in the New States," in D. Wall, ed., *Chicago Essays on Economic Development* (Chicago: University of Chicago Press, 1972), pp. 23–40.

4. George Macesich, *The International Monetary Economy and the Third World* (New York: Praeger, 1981), Chaps. 1–2.

5. For a discussion of bureaucracy and its various manifestations, see Francis E. Rourke, *Bureaucracy, Politics, and Public Policy*, 2d ed. (Boston: Little, Brown, 1976); James Q. Wilson, "The Rise of the Bureaucratic State," *The Public Interest* 41 (Fall 1975), pp. 77–103; Anthony Downs, *Inside Bureaucracy* (Boston: Little, Brown, 1967); Harold Seidman, *Politics, Position, and Power: The Dynamics of Federal Organization*, 3d ed. (New York: Oxford University Press, 1980); I. M. Destler, *Presidents, Bureaucrats, and Public Policy* (Princeton: Princeton University Press, 1975); Donald P. Warwick, *A Theory of Public Bureaucracy* (Cambridge, Mass.: Harvard University Press, 1975); David B. Walker, *Toward a Functioning Federalism* (Cambridge, Mass.: Winthrop, 1981); James G. Marc and Herbert A. Simon, *Organizations* (New York: Wiley, 1958); Herbert A. Simon, *Administrative Behavior*, 3d ed. (New York: Free Press, 1976); Aaron Wildavsky, *The Politics of the Budgetary Process*, 2d ed. (Boston: Little, Brown, 1974); Samuel Krislov, *Representative Bureaucracy* (Englewood Cliffs, N.J.: Prentice Hall, 1974); George J.Gordon, *Public Administration in America*, 2d ed. (New York: St. Martin's Press, 1982); Max Weber, *On Charisma and Institution Building—Selected Papers*, ed. with an introduction by S. M. Eisenstadt (Chicago: University of Chicago Press, 1968).

6. Robert A. Solo, *The Positive State* (Cincinnati: South-Western Publishing Company, 1982), p. 57; and M. M. Clark, *Social Control of Business*, 2d ed. (New York: McGraw-Hill, 1939), pp. 95–96.

7. Solo, *Positive State*, p. 57.

8. Solo, *Positive State*, p. 59.

9. Solo, *Positive State*, p. 59.

10. George Macesich, *The Politics of Monetarism: Its Historical and Institutional Development* (Totowa, N.J.: Rowman and Allanheld, 1984), pp. 16–38.

11. Robert A. Solo, "The Neo-Marxist Theory of the State," *Journal of Economic Issues* 12: 4 (December 1978), pp. 829–42.

12. George Macesich, *Economic Nationalism and Stability* (New York: Praeger, 1985), especially Chap. 2.

13. George Macesich, *Monetary Reform and Cooperation Theory* (New York: Praeger, 1989).

14. Wildavsky, *Politics of the Budgetary Process*, pp. 189–94.

15. Wildavsky, *Politics of the Budgetary Process*, p. 192.

16. Downs, *Inside Bureaucracy*, Chap. 8.

17. Gordon, *Public Administration*, Chap. 1.

6

Property Rights, Privatization, and Other Issues

JUDICIAL STATE

Market democracy in its theoretical ideal is a minimal and primarily juridical state, which has no value other than to facilitate and protect the individual pursuit of personal values and private ends. It is subordinate to, and intended only to protect the security and property of, the individual. For this purpose it lays down and enforces rules for the exercise of property power, lest the freedom of one transgress upon the freedom of another. It must draw boundaries on the rights of property, lest the claims of one trespass on the prerogatives of another. It must provide for the interpretation and enforcement of contracts voluntarily entered into by private parties in the process of exchanges.

PROPERTY RIGHTS AND THEIR IMPORTANCE

The concept of property rights typically involves various rights that are put together in a market democracy. These include

- The right to use property for personal use, including consumption and production
- The right to receive proceeds from property rental
- The right to sell fixed and variable equity shares in an established enterprise
- The right to establish and liquidate enterprise[1]

These rights are promoted from theory to practice by contractual freedom within an environment that facilitates and protects the individual pursuit of personal values and private ends. They characterize and describe the juridical nature of a market democracy.

A society's property rights are important determinants in wealth distribution. Historical evidence shows that some rights promote growth and others lead to stagnation. However, little is known about the process by which property rights are established or how they change in response to new conditions.

Studies—some serious, some otherwise—have examined the meaning of ownership and control, concepts that are so critical to the issue of property rights and their evolution over time and to changing conditions.[2] In the mid–nineteenth century, *The Economist* observed that matters were simple. Clear-cut categories existed and produced clear-cut answers to the age-old question of who gets what:

> Workers were paid a wage, managers a salary, creditors some interest. Shareholders got the rest, which was sometimes a lot and sometimes nothing, taking it out of the company as dividends or reinvesting it there. Successful entrepreneurs—Carnegie and Rockefeller in America, Krupp in Germany, Pilkington in England, Mitsui in Japan— became immensely rich. Nobody doubted who owned the typical capitalist company. The shareholders did, and they could do pretty much as they liked.[3]

As the political franchise was expanded to include more people, laws constraining the so-called Carnegie-Rockefeller phase of capitalism were passed. Antitrust laws, laws promoting unions and worker safety, and related legislation brought to a close a phase in the development of property rights.

Political factors aside, the desire by the wealthy to make their wealth more liquid, marketable, and mobile promoted the growth of shares, or stocks, and a public stock exchange. Thus, the publicly quoted company (which issued shares that could be bought and sold on a stock exchange) together with the concept of limited liability served to set in motion profound changes in the extension and deepening of property rights. In the United States, the number of industrial firms with issued shares rose from 30 in 1893 to 170 in 1897; in Britain, the rise was from 60 in 1887 to almost 600 in 1907.[4]

For all their importance in the area of property rights, stock markets are but one means available to firms for raising capital. Some firms do not deal directly with the public as such. They place extra shares privately with a select group of investors. In the United States in 1988, the amount placed in this manner amounted to more than $200 billion.

Other evidence cited by *The Economist* that suggests the changing nature of stock markets in the United States includes the apparent decline of the private investor and of buy-outs, which mostly involve a switch from equity to debt. Between the end of 1983 and the end of 1989, U.S. investors reduced their equity holdings by around $550 billion, equivalent to 40 percent of their portfolios in 1983. *The Economist* observes that, were this trend to continue, the last American to own shares directly would sell his last one in the year 2003.

The buy-out technique consists mostly of switching from equity to debt. The typical procedure is to marshal funds (usually from bank loans or by issuing bonds to banks) and to pay off the equity holders. To be sure, some investors do get an equity stake. Most, however, do not. This is the so-called junk bond market, whose growth has averaged, according to *The Economist*, 26 percent per year between 1985 and 1989.

According to *The Economist*, these trends should serve as a "simple but essential warning: in America and Britain during the 1980s, something went wrong with the standard system in which equity is king and the stock exchange its court."[5]

These appear to be but symptoms of what many view as the changing nature of ownership in the advanced industrial countries. To be sure, the legal nature of equity as representing ownership is unchanged. What apparently has changed is the functional reality of equity.[6]

This change in reality means that the typical shareholder may no longer view a share of stock as representing ownership in, say, his or her house. A share of stock now seems to represent little more than a right to a dividend or, possibly, capital appreciation. In effect, shareholders in the United States and Britain do not behave like owners. They feel powerless to influence a firm's affairs and thus do not become actively involved. There are, of course, exceptions.

Some shareholder abdication can be traced to the development of huge institutional fund investors and their managers. Dissatisfaction with a firm's performance is most easily resolved, in the view of fund managers, by simply selling the shares. This method is cheap, quick, and convenient. It does not require fund managers to become too involved with a firm's operations and how they may be improved.

The net effect has been to erode property rights in U.S. and British firms. Neither the shareholders nor even the appointed directors behave as owners of a given firm whose shares are traded on the market. This has prompted managers of the firms to step in and promote themselves as owners through various techniques, including leveraged buy-outs. The intention apparently is to rejoin the tradition of career entrepreneurs.

Indeed, the most successful economies in the world are those with firms solidly lodged in the tradition of proprietor-managers. For example, until the mid-1980s both Japan and Germany included significant proprietor-management firms in their economies. As a matter of fact, relatively few firms are publicly traded in Germany and Japan—only about one-quarter of all the shares quoted on the Tokyo exchange are available to be bought and sold. In both countries, moreover, institutional investors are traditionally less active than in the United States and Britain. Since 1985, the situation in both countries has changed; it appears to be approaching what existed in the United States and Britain during the period 1985–1990.

In essence, the basic requirement for a successful economy is a fully working system of property rights. In addition to explicit laws on who owns what, it also requires that people respect and believe in the spirit and letter of the law, and that they behave accordingly. Where the proprietary tradition is strong, the entrepreneurial spirit will thrive. Where such a spirit thrives, the best investment decisions usually ensue.

The changing structure of firms in the United States and Britain, and very likely elsewhere, is confirmed by *The Economist*.[7] The trends do suggest a moving away from institutional investors toward a proprietary form of ownership. This suggests a closer identity of interest between shareholders and managers. It may also mean substantial ownership by managers. All of this suggests that firms will be better and more efficiently run. The more effective the firm and its operations, the better for the economy of the country. When combined with relentless competition, owner-entrepreneurship does provide a vibrant combination for successful economic growth and prosperity.

PRIVATIZATION

The importance of property rights makes it all the more critical for the former socialist countries of Eastern Europe to be successful in their attempts to forge market democracies out of the scrap metal of socialism. These countries have yet to come to grips with this most critical task: transferring state enterprises to private owners.[8]

The daunting scale and prodigious difficulties of the undertaking make the privatizations conducted by Margaret Thatcher's government in Britain look trivial by comparison. It took Britain seven years to sell off forty-three state-run corporations. Poland, on the other hand, aims to place 8,000 firms in private hands in three to five years. The big question, of course, is how to privatize equitably and efficiently in a country with no stock or bond market, no private banks, and no accounting system.

The strategy used in the West whereby the best state enterprises are sold one by one through public stock offer would be very difficult to employ in the East. In the first place, deciding what each firm is worth would in itself be difficult. In the second place, the availability of private domestic capital in these countries is very scarce. Third, there is considerable danger that each privatization would marshal more opposition from the remaining state-enterprise workers who fear losing their jobs.

Under these circumstances, some people would ignore the problem of valuing firms altogether and would auction off shares in state-owned firms as rapidly as possible. The net result would very likely be that the government would have to (1) accept very low prices for these firms from nationals with cash or (2) sell much of the state industry to foreign investors. Such a venture could have very serious political consequences for the government.

In order to avoid these complications, various proposals have been made that the governments simply turn the people's property back to the people. In Poland, advisors have a strategy that would give 10 percent of the shares gratis to workers in firms. An additional 5 percent would go to managers as part of incentive compensation packages. Twenty percent would go to the 25 million adult Poles. These shares would, in effect, be placed in closed and mutual funds whose stock would be distributed free to the public.[9]

Another 20 percent would be allocated to newly formed private pension funds from which workers would receive pensions. This would allow the government to reduce its social security obligations. Another 20 percent would be used to recapitalize existing state-owned commercial banks and insurance companies. The remaining 25 percent would be sold by the government to domestic purchasers and foreigners.

To be sure, the Polish plan would deprive the government of revenue it could have received if it sold shares. On the other hand, giveaways speed up the process of assigning private rights to owners so that firms can immediately begin to operate more efficiently. Such a strategy also avoids large windfall gains and losses that could create serious inequalities in income. Moreover, by allowing pension funds, mutual funds, and banks into the action, the whole process can be monitored more effectively and efficiently in terms of the operations of newly established private corporations.

Hungary has envisioned a process of privatization based on three major laws.[10] The first, a so-called Company Act, focused on the ways and means to establish new firms. This was followed by the Act of Transformation, which determined how state-owned firms may be operated under the new terms of partnership by drawing in foreign or private capital. Both laws, however, stopped short of providing explicit statements on property rights and establishing clearly who was authorized to make decisions about the sale of state property.

In the case of firms directly controlled by ministries, the matter is straightforward: The responsible ministries can undertake the processes of privatization. Problems do arise, however. Since the mid-1980s, most Hungarian firms have been operated by a management-type council. These have exercised property rights on behalf of the state. The abuses encouraged by such an arrangement (e.g., promoting short-term firm and council interests at the expense of the general public's and state's interests) soon became clear.

To avoid such problems, the Hungarian parliament passed a law establishing the State Asset Handling Agency. Its responsibility is to direct the process of privatization. This includes vetoing the decisions of firm councils if, in its opinion, such decisions are contrary to Hungarian national interests.

The party that heads the Hungarian government coalition at present has decided to sell twenty state-owned firms to private owners through shares. These twenty firms account for about 1 percent of the state property. In addition, 10,000 small firms are slated for privatization. Approximately 2,000 to 3,000 of these firms have been under a special arrangement that gives them a semi-private status. There are also efforts under way for the government and National Board to provide loans for the establishment of 20,000 to 30,000 new private firms.

For its part, the Czechoslovak government is encouraging the privatization of shops, services, and restaurants dealing directly with the public. It is anticipated that people whose property was confiscated after 1948 will have the right to reclaim it. At this writing, compensation rules are still to be worked out. Up to 70,000 small firms are involved.

In a second phase, 70 to 80 percent of the large state-owned firms will be sold. At this point it is unclear how foreign investors may participate. A third phase is envisioned in which state-run firms will be sold to the public through vouchers that will later be transferred into shares.

The Rumanian government published its privatization bill at the end of October 1990. The new law allows full ownership of firms by foreign investors. Half of the country's state-owned assets are to be sold over the period 1990–1993. Priorities for sale represent the areas of agriculture, food industry, light industry, housing construction, service, tourism, trade, and transport.

Bulgaria has no specific plans on how and when to privatize agriculture and land ownership. The government announced in the closing months of 1990 that it wants to bring about fifty bills into parliament that will turn the state-owned economy into a Western-style market economy.

Privatization thus continues to be a serious problem for the former socialist countries. It has trailed behind other reforms.

The fact is that no one knows how to privatize a centralized economy for the simple reason that it has never been done. The Soviet Union's Shatalin Plan, named after the chairman of the committee that drafted it, is but a case in point. It would convert state property into private property. Unfortunately, it provides no specifics on how this is to be done. One possibility would be to sell firms to the highest bidder. But how does the state sell property when there are no market prices to guide choices? If people found that they had paid more for property than it was worth—and there would be many—they would be bitter indeed. That could be fatal in a country whose government so far rules without a popular mandate.

Another possibility, as we have noted, would be to give away the properties, thereby avoiding the need to establish fair prices. Every citizen would start off on the same basis; no one could claim foul. Of course, there is a flaw here, too. If everyone owned the firms, no one would have a big enough stake to control them. This would constitute private ownership without private accountability.

In effect, the managers would be free to do as they pleased. In Poland, managers were said to be writing sweetheart deals with foreign investors: The foreigners got the companies for cheap and the managers got rich. Privatization only sounds simple; there are very big gaps between intentions, actions, and results.

Thanks to their country's worker-management system, Yugoslavs are perhaps in the best position to make privatization take hold. Various suggestions for quickly privatizing the Yugoslav firms have been made. One particularly important approach has been suggested by Marshall R. Colberg, and a similar one has been made by Milton Friedman. Essentially, both would turn over equity shares to worker-managers and thereby provide them with private property rights in the firm. A recently established stock exchange would be empowered to trade in these equities.[11]

The transition to market democracy from socialism obviously involves a political transition as well. Many questions will be raised during the transition period in these countries, and time alone will answer them. It is clear that half-measures grafting market elements onto a basically socialist system do not work. It is also clear that it is one thing to pronounce support for radical reform, and quite another to pull it off.

NOTES

1. For a useful summary of issues involving property rights, see Eirik Furubotn and Svetozar Pejovich, eds., *The Economics of Property Rights* (Cambridge, Mass.: Ballinger Publishing, 1974); Harold Demsetz, "Towards a Theory of Property Rights," *American Economic Review* (May 1967), pp. 347-59.

2. "Capitalism: Survey," *The Economist* (May 5, 1990), pp. 5-20.

3. "Capitalism: Survey," p. 7.

4. "Capitalism: Survey," p. 7.

5. "Capitalism: Survey," p. 8.

6. "Capitalism: Survey," p. 8.

7. "Capitalism: Survey," pp. 5-20.

8. For a discussion of issues involved in privatization, see L. Gray Cowan, *Privatization in the Developing World* (New York: Praeger, 1990).

9. Sylvia Nasar, "Privatization: If You Can't Sell It, Give It Away," *U.S. News and World Report* (October 1, 1990), p. 73.

10. Zsuzsa Ban, "Privatization: Not without Its Problems," *Hungarian Trade Journal* (July-August 1990), p. 6.

11. Marshall R. Colberg, "Property Rights and Motivation: UNited States and Yugoslavia," *Proceedings and Reports*, Center for Yugoslav-American Studies, Research, and Exchanges, The Florida State University, Vol. 12-13 (1978-1979), pp. 52-58; Milton Friedman in an interview with Drago Baum in *Privredni Vjesnik* (February 15, 1990); George Macesich, ed., with the assistance of R. Lang, L. Markovic, and D. Vojnic, *Yugoslavia in the Age of Democracy: Essays on Economic and Political Reform* (Praeger, forthcoming).

7

The Politics of Reform

OBSTACLES TO REFORM

The move by Eastern European countries from central planning toward free markets appears to be a slow, difficult, and socially divisive transition. It would seem that it is easier to institute political reform in these countries than to institute serious economic reform. Indeed, in some countries there is recognition that policy changes may already be running ahead of public attitudes and that a state-controlled system in place for four decades will not be easily displaced.

Despite the obvious obstacles and public resistance in some countries, a consensus is emerging in Eastern Europe about the strategies and measures that are necessary to move toward a market democracy. The basic minimum package of measures includes (1) abolishing most price controls, (2) slashing subsidies to consumers and industry, (3) giving firms autonomy, (4) ending monopolies, (5) permitting workers to be laid off, (6) accepting bankruptcies, and (7) moving toward a convertible currency.

For all the talk of free markets, however, the vision of a better future in many of these countries often appears to bear more resemblance to a Swedish-style social democracy with its generous welfare benefits than to the more free-market economy of the United States. Nevertheless, there is agreement that the stagnant economies of these countries first need the therapy of market reforms in order to move their economies off top dead center. There is also agreement that all of this will take years, even decades, to complete, and that help will be needed from abroad in the form of technology and investment.

The structural obstacles to reform cannot be overstated. The sheer weight of state control in these countries and the difficulty of tilting the balance quickly to private enterprise is daunting. Throughout Eastern Europe, the state typically owns more than 95 percent of industry. Differences in the standard of living, inflation rate, debt burden, and political climate may mean differences in the economic strategies each nation adopts. In effect, the speed and specifics of each nation's reform must fit its separate requirements. It may well be that no standard model for reform exists.

Nevertheless, these countries have much to learn from each other. Their government officials and economists agree that they all need foreign investment. The steps needed to build a basic market system are similar for all the countries concerned.

1. Monetary reform is needed to ensure control of the stock of money and, ultimately, the general level of prices.

2. Fiscal control is needed to guarantee budgetary balance and to limit monetization of the budget deficit that is typical in these countries. Currency convertibility should be an integral part of reform in order to provide the economy with a realistic link to the world economy. Subsidies should be removed; wages should be decontrolled and allowed to reflect realistic demand-and-supply conditions. A safety net should be put into place to protect workers temporarily unemployed while the transformation to a market economy takes place. Privatization, with legal protection of property rights, is critical. Monopolies should be ended and serious entrepreneurial and labor incentives encouraged.

Monetary reforms should also include a thorough reorganization of the banking system. Eastern European banks have done little more than channel subsidies to inefficient firms. A solid banking system can discipline and steer resources to efficient firms and the private sector.

A convertible currency restores faith in a country's currency. At the same time, it increases incentives to work and reduces inflationary expectations. Without a convertible currency, foreign trade is usually reduced to barter, bilateral agreements, and other inefficient means of trade.

Eliminating subsidies to consumers and producers reduces distortions in the price system. All too often, subsidies to producers serve to keep inefficient firms in business. They seldom provide incentives for these firms to increase efficiency because the firms know that subsidies will be forthcoming to keep them in business. Moreover, subsidies are a very important source of a country's budgetary problems, thereby undermining fiscal control.

A visible safety net serves to provide for workers who become unemployed when firms are driven to reduce costs and increase efficiency or when they go bankrupt. Such a safety net will make the transformation to a market democracy more readily accepted by the public at large.

Ending monopolies guarantees that price and market reforms will not allow the state monopolies to simply raise prices once reforms have been introduced. These monopolies make it very difficult indeed for new firms to enter and for competition to prevail. It would be a mistake to initiate price reform while maintaining and promoting monopoly.

It is important to recognize that all the components of reforms are interactive and supportive. Thus, if prices are deregulated without at the same time establishing control of the money supply and imposing fiscal restraint, inflation and inconvertibility will follow. Moreover, if privatization and demonopolization of state industry does not take place or is postponed, the effectiveness of the reforms will be reduced, if not thwarted. If a social safety net is not in place when the reforms are launched, the reforms may be viewed as causing widespread unemployment, social stress, and political instability.

Our discussion of market democracy does explicitly recognize the interdependent nature of reform. Transformation of the socialist countries into functioning democracies with market economies depends on implementing the various components of market democracy simultaneously. One cannot simply pick and choose various components for independent implementation.

A case in point was President Gorbachev's attempt to combine central control with market reform in the Soviet Union. It was an exercise in futility when judged against our discussion of the requirements for a market democracy. Gorbachev's marriage of market and central control would leave in place controls on prices of essential consumer goods, basic commodities such as oil and gas, and services such as transportation and communications. Although budgetary restraint would be imposed, subsidies for many state enterprises would continue. No timetable for privatization is given, even though much lip service is paid to the idea. The same is true about ruble convertibility.

Even Poland's efforts at reform—admirable though they are—contain significant shortcomings. Even though partial privatization has taken place, there has been a delay in breaking up state monopolies and wage reform, which are necessary to create proper incentives for managers and workers. The result has been serious supply shortfalls and resource misallocation problems.

Why the delay in implementing reforms that are so obviously needed in these countries? In short, strong counterreform forces present formidable barriers. These forces represent a very diverse group. They range from nationalists to socialists to communists to an ever-alert bureaucracy, all of whom pay lip service to all of the elements of a market democracy. Many of these people remain entrenched in the bureaucracy and nationalist movements. Their ambivalence to reform is transparent. They seek to delay and temporize reforms for reasons we have discussed here in the chapters on nationalism and bureaucracy.

If these former socialist countries are to avoid disillusionment and easy solutions, reform and democracy must prove economically and politically more profitable than dictatorship. This is especially important in a region where nearly a dozen nationalities are crammed together in a relatively small area. These countries must prove to themselves and the rest of the world that they are able to mobilize all of their resources—human as well as natural. They do indeed possess the raw materials, transportation, energy, arable land, and a relatively educated pool of human resources.

PROMOTING REFORM AND THE YUGOSLAV EXPERIENCE

Experience with the processes of reform indicates that quality people are required to carry out quality reforms.[1] To be sure, quality politicians are in short supply the world over. Good government in democratic societies is difficult but not impossible to achieve. When the structures and incentives are right, it is possible to transform the performance of many dynamic workers who have been held back by the old system. At the same time, it is important to replace those people who cannot or will not adapt to the new environment.

When the objectives of reform are clearly defined, it is important to implement reform with speed. If the implementation is slow and hesitant, various interest groups will likely sabotage the reforms. The economy operates as an organic whole, not as an unrelated collection of bits and pieces. Moreover, costs appear immediately, whereas the benefits of reform may take twice as long to achieve. It is uncertainty, not speed, that endangers structural reform programs.

The momentum of reform must be maintained until the entire program is completed. Opponents of reform are not likely to give up their privileges and protection easily. Reforms and the government that promotes them must stay ahead to lead the public debate.

Removing privileges evenly across the board diminishes the opposition of vested-interest groups while enabling all factions to have a more constructive role in the reformed society.

It is important to maintain credibility to keep public confidence in the reform venture and to minimize the costs of the undertaking. Thus, it is essential that policy be consistent and communications open and effective. The public must be kept fully informed and must consider itself an active participant in the reform processes.

The Yugoslav experience over several decades of efforts at reform is important here. An underlying problem of the country's earlier reforms was that they lacked a national consensus of objectives. For the most part, the earlier reforms did not seriously address the crucial issues of (1) private property rights, (2) free and open markets, (3) a proper monetary and financial organization to serve a modern market economy, and (4) the important issue of multiparty policies. In terms of this last issue, the reforms missed an opportunity to promote the separation of the state and bureaucratic apparatus from single political party control.

Instead, the Yugoslavs sought reform through socialist, decentralized worker self-management. The shortcomings of such an arrangement were obvious very early in the process. I have discussed these elsewhere, as have other writers.[2] What should be underscored here is that although the workers had the right to control and manage their respective firms and had direct personal interest in the income produced, they did not own their firms. Because they could not sell the firms, they had little interest in their market value. Worker interest in a firm's revenue also leaves something to be desired, because if workers leave the firm, they cannot sell their interests in its future profits and income. Such an arrangement ensures that workers will opt for an increase in current revenue at the expense of new investments and preservation of assets. Moreover, problems are compounded by the lack of labor mobility and the disincentive on recruitment of new workers that such an arrangement promotes.

To keep these firms going and to check that worker-managers did not decapitalize the firms and force additional workers upon them, the bureaucracy expanded at all levels of the country. This guaranteed that vested interests would serve to undercut and sidetrack serious economic and political reform. At the same time, the socialist worker-managed firms were assured ready access to credit and borrowing and thus were protected from bankruptcy. This arrangement removed constraints from the workers, increasing their salaries as well as incentives to increase efficiency.

The net result has been to impart into the Yugoslav economy a highly inflationary bias. Two factors spelled trouble for the Yugoslav experiment: direct access to banks on the part of socialist worker-managers, and the National Bank's inability to impose restraint. Limitations and problems of the country's monetary and financial organization have been discussed elsewhere at length.[3]

To enact the right policies and survive the heat, a political leadership needs both political legitimacy and a supporting constituency. In the past, the Yugoslav leadership has implemented reforms piecemeal, more or less soldering various market reforms into the socialist worker-management model. This has created inflation, unemployment, and little gain. The Yugoslav model must be transformed into a real market economy. Otherwise, its experiment with socialist worker-management will become an obstacle to reform and a milepost on the road to economic disaster and potential political chaos.

Equally important in the reform process is the ongoing debate with strong nationalist and ethnic overtones over the structure and very existence of some of the reforming countries. In Yugoslavia, for example, debate focuses on whether the country should be organized as a federacy, as a confederacy or as separate republics.

In this discussion we have reviewed the likely results of nationalism. The by-products of economic nationalism in particular reduce a country's real income. Disappointment with the economy's performance on this score increasingly pushes the government into the formation of prices and wages to promote desired outcomes. Typically, this leads to wage and price controls. Because wage and price controls inevitably fail, the system is increasingly driven into collective participatory planning where wages and prices are determined. This may, in fact, be desired by some people. Nevertheless, such an arrangement offers little chance that the market system will be allowed to play its effective and efficient role.

NOTES

1. Roger Douglas, "The Politics of Successful Structural Reforms," *The Wall Street Journal* (January 17, 1990); and George Macesich, ed., with the assistance of R. Lang, L. Markovic, and D. Vojnic, *Yugoslavia in the Age of Democracy: Essays on Economic and Political Reform* (Praeger, forthcoming).

2. Chapter 6, "Workers' Management" and Chapter 7 "The Firm," in George Macesich, *Yugoslavia: Theory and Practice of Development Planning* (Charlottesville: University Press of Virginia, 1964); Rikard Lang, George Macesich, and Dragomir Vojnic, eds., *Essays on the Political Economy of Yugoslavia* (Zagreb: Informator, 1982); George Macesich, ed., with the assistance of R. Lang and D. Vojnic, *Essays on the Yugoslav Economic Model* (New York: Praeger, 1989).

3. Dimitrije Dimitrijevic and George Macesich, *Money and Finance in Contemporary Yugoslavia*, with a foreword by Milton Friedman (New York: Praeger, 1973); and Dimitrije Dimitrijevic and George Macesich, *Money and Finance in Contemporary Yugoslavia: A Comparative Analysis* (New York: Praeger, 1984).

8

Europe Re-examined

THE THEORY OF ECONOMIC INTEGRATION

Is it possible that the reforming countries of Eastern and Central Europe can put aside nationalism and prove to themselves and the rest of the world that they are able to mobilize all of their domestic resources, as well as the resources that can be organized regionally? For useful insights into an answer, we turn to the theory of economic integration and the experience of the Austro-Hungarian Empire before 1914, when many of these reforming countries were its members.

We may briefly summarize our theory of economic integration. Why do various countries, regions, and communities pursue economic integration, or at least pay lip service to it? Foremost is the belief that integration will increase economic efficiency by emphasizing lower-cost methods of production. By increasing the mobility of factors of production, as well as other goods and services, the standard of living is increased. Opportunities for individuals are increased, as are the freedom and range of alternatives available to individuals. Effects of internal-external economic fluctuations are minimized by integration.

Essentially, efforts to achieve economic integration are steps toward free trade, but only within a particular region.[1] The removal of tariffs among members of an integrated unit and their equalization against nonmembers very likely creates obstacles (in some cases greater and more formidable than previously existed) for nonmembers. Unless integration occurs among large and economically strong nations, the effect on worldwide economic efficiency is likely to be small. Indeed, integration among small and economically weak nations can actually reduce worldwide economic efficiency.

Economic integration can be brought about in a series of steps. The first step requires that participants abolish all tariffs, quotas, and any other quantitative and qualitative restrictions against the movement of goods and services across national boundaries within the area. Such an area is called a free trade area.

The second step requires the equalization by participants of all tariffs, quotas, and other quantitative and qualitative restrictions imposed against nonmember countries. This is, in effect, the creation of a customs union; it includes the creation of a common agency for the collection and disbursement of revenues among participants according to an agreed-upon formula.

The third step requires that member nations allow all factors of production, as well as goods and services, to move freely within an area. No barriers arising from the existence of national boundaries are to be placed in the path of such movement. This is, in effect, the establishment of a common market. The fourth step requires that participants harmonize their national economic and social policies with one another while still maintaining individual sovereignty. This does not require exact duplication of policies, of course, but merely agreement in the same general direction. This is, in effect, the formulation of an economic union.

Complete economic integration occurs in the fifth and final step, which requires each of the national units to delegate irrevocably the control of all social and economic policymaking to a central, federal type of agency, which then takes over all governmental economic functions.

Because the drive for economic integration appears to be motivated by desires to increase economic efficiency, it is useful to examine the variables most likely to affect efficiency in a given market area. The greater the complementarity of participating economies of a newly integrated market area, the greater (it is argued) will be the gains from union.[2] This is the consequence of increased trade, typically at the expense of the rest of the world. In effect, the union diverts trade from the rest of the world to the participating countries.

Another argument rejects the complementarity hypothesis and advances the proposition that a union of competitive economies is more promising, provided that large cost differences exist among participants.[3] Under such an arrangement, the lowest-cost producers would increase production to supply larger portions of the entire market, while the highest-cost producers would shift into the production of goods and services (for which they had a comparative cost advantage) or go out of business. In effect, a union of cost-competitive economies would create more trade among members of the union. The net effect would be to increase the economic efficiency of member countries, as well as that of the rest of the world.

Some economists argue that a union of small countries presents the best possibility because socioeconomic policy can be swiftly and accurately adjusted to changing economic conditions.[4] The presumption is that a smaller economy responds more quickly to policy changes than a larger one. A counterargument is that speed of response to policy changes is the critical assumption, not the size of participating countries. Socioeconomic policy changes can be made about as rapidly in large countries as in smaller ones. The greater the economic size of the union, moreover, the greater the elasticity of its reciprocal demand and the lesser the elasticity of the reciprocal demand of the rest of the world.[5] All other things being equal, the greater the size of the union, the greater the degree of intra-union trade and the lesser the degree of extra-union trade. As a result, the participating countries are better off and, presumably, so are their inhabitants.

Geographic proximity tends to be a positive element in economic integration. Common tastes, habits, and similar cultural and social institutions all arise from the contiguity of natural frontiers. On the other hand, this is often a source of ill feeling, which must be overcome if the full benefits of economic integration are to be realized. Assuming that a transportation system exists, shorter distances usually mean lower transportation costs. Moreover, if the union re-establishes trade relations that have been broken or reduced because of tariffs and quotas among neighboring countries, considerable increase in the economic efficiency of the participating countries will occur.

Height of tariff barriers has important effects on economic efficiency. Level of pre-union tariffs among participating countries, level of tariffs imposed on nonmember countries, level of current tariffs imposed by nonmember countries on the goods and services of member countries—all are factors to be taken into account. For example, the higher the level of pre-union tariffs, the greater the gains from integration as a consequence of favorable effects on efficiency from the removal of restrictions. In effect, the greater the move by the union in the direction of freer trade, the better it is for participating countries and the rest of the world.

Furthermore, the greater the changes in the location of production, whether within or outside the economic union, the greater the benefits that are likely from the union. Such shifting is merely an indication that enterprises are moving to lower-cost locations and are opting for lower-cost methods of production or are just putting new facilities in the right place. In any case, a greater increase in efficiency will probably be the end result.

A HISTORICAL EXAMPLE: THE AUSTRO-HUNGARIAN EMPIRE

Consider now the experience of the Austro-Hungarian Empire in light of our theory of integration. Even the first step as a free trade area was never completed in Austro-Hungary. Internal trade between the constituent provinces of the empire was treated on the same basis as foreign trade.[6] Tariffs and other trade restrictions were imposed on internal trade and, in most cases, goods paid both import and export duties. By the eighteenth century, some progress toward removal of restrictions had occurred, although goods going from Silesia to Trieste had to pay duties at six points. On the Danube route within the empire, duties on goods were paid at thirteen points. It is significant that during the eighteenth century when circumstances were particularly favorable for establishing a free trade area, new customs frontiers were established between Hungary on one side and Croatia, Slavonia, Transylvania, and Banat on the other.

The tariff of 1775 abolished all internal customs between the Austrian provinces and Hungary, except with the Tyrol. Again, the first step toward authentic economic integration was frustrated. Moreover, in 1793 import and export duties were reimposed at the Hungarian frontier for goods going either way; by 1798 most of the duties on coffee, corn, and beverages were re-established between the various parts of the empire. By 1815 the empire contained no less than seven separate customs groups—each of them separated from the rest of the empire.

Something of the idea of free trade began to seep into the empire following the Napoleonic wars. Indeed, in 1826 the customs boundary between the Tyrol and the rest of the empire was abolished. On the other hand, the customs barrier against Hungary continued. Such an arrangement was continued ostensibly as the only means at the disposal of the central authorities for taxing Hungary. The Hungarian gentry refused to pay taxes. This is mute testimony to the viability of the Austro-Hungarian economy.

After more than 300 years of political union, Austria and Hungary were joined into an economic unit in 1850. Even so, the action cannot be considered as representing integration theory. From 1850 to about 1914, participants in the so-called Austro-Hungarian customs union paid more attention to wrecking each other's trade than to actively promoting free trade.

The Tyrol continued to collect customs duties, while Dalmatia imposed duties and tariffs on grain and flour imported from other parts of the empire.[7] Bohemia discouraged the consumption of Hungarian flour, while Hungary discouraged the purchase of goods manufactured outside Hungary. In effect, the empire fell far short of achieving complete economic integration. Even the first step—that of moving toward such integration—was not completed.

If we examine the variables most likely to promote economic efficiency and to encourage economic integration of the Austro-Hungarian Empire, we find that they were largely ineffective, if not completely at odds with economic integration. In the first place, these lands were not complementary to one another nor did large cost differences exist among them. Natural endowment, for example, did not necessarily favor the industrialization of western provinces such as Bohemia-Moravia, Silesia, Lower and Upper Austria, and Lower and Upper Styria. Similar resources could also be found in the South Slavic and Rumanian territories. To a great extent the same is true when considerations of agriculture are taken into account. In terms of natural resources as well as human resources, every national group had about equal chances for developing its respective economy quite independently of other areas of the empire. Thus, for example, it is important to note that by 1910 the foreign trade of Austria and Hungary separately achieved greater significance than trade between the two areas.[8]

This does not mean that a basis for trade between the various areas of the empire did not exist. From received doctrine, the theory of comparative advantage is a static argument for a country to specialize in the production of commodities that require the use of its relatively abundant factor. The static nature of the theory, however, does not invalidate its use in countries undergoing economic development. Changing conditions merely provide a new basis for comparative advantage. For example, if capital accumulation proceeds faster in one country than in others, the factor endowments underlying comparative advantage itself change. The basis for trade is changed. However, a new basis does exist.

Furthermore, the opponents of comparative advantage must overcome the preference given by the theory of specialization. Received theory argues that, ceteris paribus, an incremental balanced unit of resources ought to be allocated to the export industries in the broad sense rather than to the import-competing industries because the country is more efficient in the production of export commodities. As a result, more of the import goods can be obtained by producing the export goods and by trading.

Inability to grasp the significance of these conclusions led the various nations within the empire into colorful, if absurd, movements—for example, the widespread "tulip" movement in Hungary. Members of the movement wore tulips on their lapels as a sign that they were boycotting all manufacturers not producing in Hungary. This, of course, was aimed principally at Austrian manufacturers. Such manifestations reinforced by competition for industrial development (as between the Alpine and Sudet regimes, for example), when coupled with similar demands of other regimes, cost out the more rational prescriptions of the doctrine of comparative advantage and the theory of specialization.

The evidence suggests that a union of relatively small countries does not necessarily present the best possibility for economic integration. This statement is not conclusive, however, just because of the Austro-Hungarian Empire's pathological relations with its neighbors on the southeastern frontier. It had apparently never occurred to the Austro-Hungarians that if steps toward full and authentic economic organization were to take place, friendly cooperation among the empire's subject nations would be required—as well as cooperation with their kinsmen on the outside. By soliciting the aid of Rumania to help drive a wedge between the North and South Slavs, the empire hoped to enlist Rumanian cooperation for economic integration. Consider also the empire's intimidation of the Serbian government in the Pig War, or its insistence that the Serbian government abandon the customs union between Serbia and Bulgaria—an event that could have been of considerable significance to the Balkan lands and to Europe.

Geographic proximity was not a favorable factor in economic integration in Austro-Hungary. Not only was the empire unable to achieve friendly cooperation with its neighbors, but the geographic proximity of various peoples within the empire did not necessarily result in common tastes, habits, and similar cultural and social institutions. In fact, several national groups comprising the empire's population did not possess similar tastes, habits, or preferences. As a result, a large consumer market for mass-produced goods and services did not exist. Much of the population persisted in wearing its own national costumes and thereby deprived the empire as a whole of specialization and economics of scale.

Transportation is another area where we would expect that geographic proximity would play an active role toward integration. In fact, an adequate and relatively inexpensive transportation system did not exist. This was symptomatic of the fact that the empire did not constitute an economic unit. The natural barriers to construction of an economically sound transportation system were simply compounded by national and state jealousies. The Dalmatian railroads are an example.[9] Dalmatia was separated from the other Austrian provinces by the Croatian territory belonging to the Hungarian kingdom. Because the proposed railway would cross Hungarian territory, permission of the Hungarian parliament was required for its building. The Hungarians opposed the railroad for fear it would make the possession of Dalmatia easier for Austria. The railroad was not built, and goods from Austria to Dalmatia were transported by rail to Trieste and from there by ship to a Dalmation port, where they were then most likely reloaded on a train.

Austro-Hungary's inability to develop the Danube into a significant economic waterway is yet another illustration that geographic proximity did not mean lower transportation costs. The building and operation of the canal at the Iron Gates in the Danube provided an excellent opportunity to weld the various nations of the empire into a cohesive economic unit, while at the same time favorably influencing economic development in all of Central and Southeastern Europe. Unfortunately, the canal tolls were discriminatory and were ten times higher than those at the Kiel Canal (which cost five times as much to construct), and its towage dues were three times higher, although the former was 96 kilometers long and the latter less than 2 kilometers.[10]

The transportation problem on the canal and the Danube was further complicated by the ridiculous and irritating requirement that Magyar was to be the sole administrative language—although one bank was partly Rumanian and the other wholly Serbian, and the traffic international. The net result, of course, was that the states on the lower Danube found it cheaper and simpler to divert heavy traffic to the sea routes. It also underscored to the Rumanians and the South Slavs (within and outside the empire) the necessity of sparing no effort in developing their territories along autonomous lines.

Since the empire was not an authentic economic unit, we should expect that opportunities for individuals and the range of alternatives available to them were limited. This is a manifestation of reduced factor mobility, whose consequence is a reduction in the standard of living. Barriers to such mobility arose principally from German-Magyar hegemony within the empire. With minor exceptions, this hegemony kept the bulk of the key positions in economic, cultural, political and social life in the hands of the Germans and Magyars. Slavs, Rumanians, and others typically provided a convenient source of raw material for Germanization or Magyarization—or simply abuse.

The absurdity and futility of German and Magyar nationalism is just as we would have expected from our earlier discussion of nationalism. Consider the data contained in the 1910 Census of Population.[11] Austro-Hungary had a total population of about 52 million in 1910. The Germans constituted 23 percent; Magyars, 20 percent; others, 5 percent. In effect, 48 percent of the population was, for all practical purposes, excluded from the mainstream of life. In Austria proper, for example, of a total of eight universities, the Germans possessed five; the Czechs, one; the Poles, two; while for the Serbo-Croats, Slovenes, Italians, Rumanians, and others, the sum total was zero. In Hungary, the situation was even worse and indicated very clearly the Magyar-driven hegemony.

As we would expect from our discussion of nationalism, the best positions were allocated by nationality. In Hungary, for example, the Magyars, while constituting slightly more than half of the population, accounted for better than 90 percent of the total employed as state officials, county officials, judges, prosecutors, lawyers, teachers, professors, and physicians in 1913.

The army is considered by some to be full of opportunities for advancement for competent and enterprising individuals irrespective of nationality, but the data do not support such a claim. In 1910, at least 85 percent of the officers were German, although the army itself consisted of better than one-half Slavs and other nationalities, excluding Magyars.

Even in the Military Frontier (1521–1871), or *Vojna Krajina*, which is considered a unique institution in the empire because of its direct allegiance to the emperor, the lot of the soldier-farmers *(granicari)* was indeed a sorry one. These soldier-farmers, consisting mostly of Serbo-Croats, witnessed their lands confiscated and turned into military preserves; their interests and their persons were abused throughout the hundreds of years in which they served as a bulwark against the onslaught of the Ottomans into Europe. At the same time, they also provided manpower for the empire's many senseless and futile wars. For their efforts, all kinds of cultural, economic, and political wrongs were inflicted upon them.[12] Consider, for example, the numerous attempts to forcibly convert the Orthodox Serbs to Roman Catholicism whenever Ottoman pressure on the frontiers subsided. Lack of schools, as well as lack of economic and political opportunities, forced upon the inhabitants of the area an abysmally low standard of living. In effect, recent research indicates that these soldier-farmers were not the enthusiastic supporters of the empire that some people would have us believe.[13] On the other hand, they did not desire to become serfs of the Croat and Roman Catholic Church estates. For them, the Frontier constituted the lesser of two evils.

Although (1) lack of multilingualism, (2) virulent nationalism bred in part by various attempts at Germanization and Magyarization, and (3) religious bigotry severely restricted the mobility of much of the empire's human capital, other capital possessed relatively greater mobility. The focal point of such capital was Vienna, whence it flowed to other parts of the empire. Gains that the economy did make can probably be attributed to a considerable extent to the operation of the Viennese capital market. Its very success, however, has brought charges by some nationalists that Viennese capitalists treated the remainder of the empire as colonies. At that time, the interest was more in turning a quick profit than in making a lasting contribution to an area's economic development.

CONCLUSION

Economic integration is little more than a compromise between free trade and protectionism. If it is true that free trade among a few nations increases their economic efficiency, it is also true that complete free trade among all nations increases the economic efficiency of the entire world. However, advocates of regional economic integration would argue that few nations are completely committed, even in principle, to free trade. Most subscribe to some form of protectionism. Accordingly, it is easier to promote economic integration on a regional level and free trade within the integrated regional unit.

The Austro-Hungarian Empire, on the other hand, is an excellent illustration that regionalism does not necessarily promote authentic economic integration or free trade. The example suggests that it is just as easy to promote worldwide free trade as it is to promote it on a regional level. The former is preferable. The advantages of worldwide free trade would flow to many nations, not simply to select members of a regional club. Also, worldwide trade would increase the efficiency within any given regional unit. It would dispense with the necessity of setting up new, expensive, and cumbersome institutions designed to serve a given region. Furthermore, antagonism among national groups would be minimized because each would be able to develop according to its own lights and within the framework of the world economy without being subject to coercive and restrictive pressures from a major or minor national group within the region.

I have discussed elsewhere an alternative arrangement to the tight bureaucratic regionalism advocated by some people. This alternative involves creating a common market of economically, politically, ethnically, and socially diverse countries or societies by means of flexible exchange rates.[14] Mistakes and successes in their respective internal policies, including property rights and free markets, would be quickly reflected in the exchange rates between them. None would be able to inflict their mistakes on the others.

NOTES

1. For a discussion of economic integration, see Bela Belassa, *The Theory of Economic Integration* (Homewood, Ill. : Richard D. Irwin, 1961); James Meade, *Problem of Economic Union* (Chicago: University of Chicago Press, 1953); Paul Streeten, *Economic Integration: Aspects and Problems* (Leyden, Holland: A. W. Sythoff, 1961); Jacob Viner, *The Customs Union Issue* (New York: Carnegie Endowment for International Peace, 1950); George Macesich, "Theory of Economic Integration and Experience of the Balkan and Danubian Countries before 1914," *Florida State University Slavic Papers*, Center for Yugoslav-American Studies, Research, and Exchanges, Florida State University, Vol. 1 (1967), pp. 11–18.

2. Belassa, *Theory of Economic Integration*, pp. 26–91.

3. Viner, *Customs Union Issue*, p. 51.

4. Belassa, *Theory of Economic Integration*.

5. Viner, *Customs Union Issue*.

6. Oscar Jaszi, *The Dissolution of the Habsburg Monarchy* (Chicago: University of Chicago Press, Third Impression, 1964); and David Mitrany, *The Effect of the War in Southeastern Europe* (New Haven: Yale University Press, 1936).

7. Jaszi, *Dissolution of the Habsburg Monarchy*, p. 191. In spite of these new interferences, trade in the empire did flourish, if only because interferences in trade after 1850 were less than before. It may be noted, however, that worldwide trade also flourished during this period.

8. Jaszi, *Dissolution of the Habsburg Monarchy*, p. 192.

9. Jaszi, *Dissolution of the Habsburg Monarchy*, p. 190.

10. Mitrany, *Effect of the War*, p. 44.

11. Jaszi, *Dissolution of the Habsburg Monarchy*, p. 271.

12. See the research on the subject presented by Gunther E. Rotuenberg, *The Military Frontier in Croatia, 1740–1881* (Chicago: University of Chicago Press, 1966) and, also by Rotuenberg, *The Austrian Military Border in Croatia, 1522–1747* (Urbana: University of Illinois Press, 1960).

13. See Rotuenberg, *Military Frontier* and *Austrian Military Border*.

14. George Macesich, *Geldpolitik in einem gemeinsamen europäischen markt* (Money in a common-market setting) (Baden-Baden: Nomos Verlagsgesellschaft, 1972); George Macesich, "Money and a Common Market: Lessons from an Early American Experience," in *Problemi privrednog razvoja i privrednog sistems jugoslavije* (Problems of economic development and the economic system of Yugoslavia), Dragomir Vojnic, Zvonimir Baletic, and Ante Cicin-Sain, et al., eds. (Zagreb: Globus, 1989), pp. 410–23.

Bibliography

Allen, W. R. "Irving Fisher, FDR, and the Great Depression." *History of Political Economy* (Winter 1977): 560–87.

Bagehot, Walter. *Lombard Street*, 1873.

Ban, Zsuzsa. "Privatization: Not without Its Problems." *Hungarian Trade Journal* (July/August 1990): 6.

Baron, S. W. *Modern Nationalism and Religion.* New York: Harper, 1947.

Becker, Gary S. *The Economics of Discrimination.* Chicago: University of Chicago Press, 1957.

Belassa, Bela. *The Theory of Economic Integration.* Homewood, Ill.: Richard D. Irwin, 1961.

Bleiberg, R. M., and J. Grant. "For Real Money: The Dollar Should Be as Good as Gold." Editorial commentary in *Barron's* (June 15, 1981).

Bordo, M. D. "The Classical Gold Standard: Some Lessons for Today." *Review*, Federal Reserve Bank of St. Louis (May 1981): 1–16.

Breton, Albert. "The Economics of Nationalism." *Journal of Political Economy* 72 (1964): 376–86.

Bronfenbrenner, Martin. "The Currency-Choice Defense." *Challenge* (January/February 1980): 31–36.

Brozen, Yale. "Minimum Wages and Household Workers." *Journal of Law and Economics* (October 1962).

Buchanan, James. "Politics, Policy and the Pigovian Margins." *Economics* (October 1960): 1–44.

_____. *The Demand and Supply of Public Goods.* Chicago: Rand McNally, 1968.

_____. "Socialism is Dead: Leviathan Lives." *Wall Street Journal* (July 18, 1990): A10.

Buchanan, James, and Gordon Tullock. *The Calculus of Consent.* Ann Arbor: University of Michigan Press, 1962.

Cantillon, Richard. *Essai sur la nature du commerce en général.* 1730–1734.

Carr, E. H. *Nationalism and After.* New York: Macmillan, 1945.

Clark, M. M. *Social Control of Business.* 2d ed. New York: McGraw-Hill, 1939.

Coase, Ronald H. "The Problem of Social Cost." *Journal of Law and Economics* (October 1960): 1–45.

Colberg, Marshall R. "Minimum Wage Effects on Florida's Economic Development." *Journal of Law and Economics* (October 1960).

———. "Property Rights and Motivation: United States and Yugoslavia." *Florida State University Proceedings and Reports.* Center for Yugoslav-American Studies, Research, and Exchanges. Vol. 12–13 (1978–1979): 52–58.

Commons, John R. *The Economics of Collective Action.* New York: Macmillan, 1950.

Cowan, L. Gray. *Privatization in the Developing World.* New York: Praeger, 1990.

Culbertson, John M. *Macroeconomic Theory and Stabilization Policy.* New York: McGraw-Hill, 1968.

Demsetz, Harold. "Towards a Theory of Property Rights." *American Economic Review* (May 1967): 347–59.

Destler, I. M. *Presidents, Bureaucrats, and Public Policy.* Princeton: Princeton University Press, 1975.

Deutch, K. W. *Nationalism and Social Communication: An Inquiry into the Foundations of Nationality.* New York: John Wiley, 1953.

Deutch, K. W., and W. J. Poltz, eds. *Nation-Building.* New York: Atherton, 1963.

Doob, L. W. *Patriotism and Nationalism: Their Psychological Foundations.* New Haven: Yale University Press, 1964.

Dorfman, J. *The Economic Mind in American Civilization.* Vol. 3. New York: Viking Press, 1949.

Douglas, Roger, "The Politics of Successful Structural Reforms." *Wall Street Journal* (January 17, 1990).

Downs, Anthony. *An Economic Theory of Democracy.* New York: Harper, 1957.

———. *Inside Bureaucracy.* Chap. 8. Boston: Little, Brown, 1967.

Earle, E. M., ed. *Nationalism and Internationalism: Essays Inscribed to Carlton J. A. Hayes.* New York: Columbia University Press, 1950.

Eban, A. *The Tide of Nationalism.* New York: Horizon Press, 1959.

Economist. "Report of the U.S. Gold Commission studying greater role for gold in the United States". (September 5, 1981): 11–12.

———. (September 19, 1981): 17–18.

_____. (May 5, 1990): 5–20.

Frankel, Jacob A. "Adjustment Lags versus Information Lags: A 'Comment' and 'Reply' by Charles R. Nelson." *Journal of Money, Credit,* and *Banking* (November 1981): 490–96.

Frankel, S. Herbert. *Two Philosophies of Money: The Conflict of Trust and Authority.* New York: St. Martin's Press, 1977: 4–6, 86–89, and 92–95.

Friedman, Milton. "Lectures in Price Theory." Mimeographed, University of Chicago, 1955.

_____. *A Program for Monetary Stability.* New York: Fordham University Press, 1959.

_____. "The Role of Monetary Policy." In *The Optimum Quantity of Money and Other Essays.* Chicago: Aldine Publishing, 1969: 99.

_____. "The Keynes Centenary: A Monetarist Reflects." *The Economist* (June 4, 1983): 19.

_____. Interview with Drago Baum in *Privredni vjesnik* (February 15, 1990).

Friedman, Milton, and Rose Friedman. *Free to Choose.* New York: Avon Books, 1981.

_____. *Tyranny of the Status* Quo. Orlando, Fla.: Harcourt Brace Jovanovich, 1984.

Friedman, Milton, and Anna J. Schwartz. *Monetary History of the United States, 1867–1960.* Princeton: Princeton University Press for National Bureau of Economic Research, 1963.

_____. *Monetary Trends in the United States and United Kingdom: Their Relationship to Revenue, Prices, and Interest Rates, 1867–1975.* Chicago: University of Chicago Press, 1982.

Furubotn, Eirik, and Svetozar Pejovich, eds. *The Economics of Property Rights.* Cambridge, Mass.: Ballinger Publishing, 1974.

Galbraith, John K. "Came the Revolution." Review of Keynes's *General Theory. New York Times Book Review* (May 16, 1965).

Gibbons, H. A. *Nationalism and Internationalism.* New York: Stokes, 1930.

Gladbe, Fred R., and Dwight R. Lee. *Microeconomics: Theory and Applications.* New York: Harcourt Brace Jovanovich, 1980.

Gooch, G. P. *Nationalism.* New York: Harcourt Brace and Howe, 1920.

Gordon, George J. *Public Administration in America.* 2d ed. Chap. 1. New York: St. Martin's Press, 1982.

Hamilton, E. J., A. Rees, and H. G. Johnson, eds. *Landmarks in Political Economy.* Selections from the *Journal of Political Economy.* Chicago: University of Chicago Press, 1962.

Hayek, F. A. *Denationalization of Money.* London: Institute of Economic Affairs, 1976.

_____. "The Keynes Centenary: The Austrian Critique." *The Economist* (June 11, 1983): 39–41.

Hayes, C. J. H. *The Historical Evolution of Modern Nationalism.* New York: R. R. Smith, 1931.

Hertz, F. O. *Nationality in History and Politics.* New York: Oxford University Press, 1944.

Hicks, John. "The Keynes Centenary: A Skeptical Follower." *The Economist* (June 18, 1983): 17–19.

Hinsley, F. H. *Nationalism and the International System.* London: Hodder and Staughton, 1973.

Hirschman, Albert. "Rival Interpretations of Market Society: Civilizing, Destructive, or Feeble?" *Journal of Economic Literature* (December 1982): 1463–84.

Hobson, John. *Work and Wealth Incentives in the New Industrial Order,* 1921.

_____. *Evolution of Modern Capitalism and Imperialism.* 1926.

_____. *Physiology of Industry.* 1956.

Hume, David. "Of Interest; Of Money," In *Essays, Moral, Political, and Literary.* Vol. 1 of *Essays and Treatises.* Edinburgh: Bell and Bradfute, Cadell, and Davis, 1804.

Hunt, E. K. *History of Economic Thought: A Critical Perspective.* Belmont, Calif.: Wadsworth, 1979.

Jaszi, Oscar. *The Dissolution of the Habsburg Monarchy.* Chicago: University of Chicago Press, 1929; third impression, 1964.

Johnson, Harry G., ed. *Economic Nationalism in Old and New States.* Chicago: University of Chicago Press, 1967.

_____. "The Ideology of Economic Policy in the New States." In *Chicago Essays on Economic Development,* ed. D. Wall. Chicago: University of Chicago Press, 1972.

Keynes, J. M. *Economic Consequences of Peace.* London: Macmillan, 1920.

_____. *A Tract on Monetary Reform.* Macmillan, 1923 and 1929.

_____. *Treatise on Money.* 1930.

_____. "A Short View of Russia." In *Essays in Persuasion.* New York: Harcourt, Brace, 1932: 306–9.

_____. *The General Theory of Employment, Interest, and Money.* New York: Harcourt, Brace, and World, First Harbinger Ed., 1964.

Kindleberger, Charles P. *Economic Development.* New York: McGraw-Hill, 1958.

Knight, Frank H. *Economic Organization.* Chicago: University of Chicago Press, 1933.

_____. *The Ethics of Competition.* New York: Augustus M. Kelley, 1950.

Kohn, Hans. *The Idea of Nationalism.* New York: Macmillan, 1944.

Krislov, Samuel. *Representative Bureaucracy.* Englewood Cliffs, N.J.: Prentice-Hall, 1974.

Laidler, David, and Nickolas Rowe. Review of S. Herbert Frankel's study, *Two Philosophies of Money: The Conflict of Trust and Authority.* In *Journal of Economic Literature* (June 1979): 570–72.

———. "Georg Simmel's *Philosophy of Money:* A Review Article for Economists." *Journal of Economic* Literature (March 1980): 97–105.

Law, John. *Money and Trade Consider'd; With a Proposal for Supplying the Nation with Money.* 1705; 2d ed., 1720.

Lehrman, E., and Henry S. Reuss. "Should the U.S. Return to the Gold Standard?" *Christian Science Monitor* (September 21, 1981).

Lucas, Robert E., Jr. "Rules, Discretion, and the Role of the Economic Advisor." In *Rational Expectations and Economic Policy,* ed. S. Fischer. Chicago: University of Chicago Press, 1980: 199–210.

Macesich, George. "Are Wage Differentials Resilient? An Empirical Test." *Southern Economic Journal* (April 1961).

———. "Current Inflation Theory: Consideration of Methodology." *Social Research* (Autumn 1961): 321–30.

———. *Commercial Banking and Regional Development in the United States: 1950–60.* Tallahassee, Fla.: Florida State University Press, 1963.

———. *Yugoslavia: The Theory and Practice of Development Planning.* Charlottesville: University of Virginia, 1964.

———. "The Theory of Economic Integration and the Experience of the Balkan and Danubian Countries before 1914." *Proceedings of the First International Congress on Southeast European Studies.* Sofia, Bulgaria (1966), and *The Florida State University Slavic Papers.* Vol. 1 (1967).

———. "Economic Theory and the Austro-Hungarian Ausgleich of 1867." In *Der Österreichisch-ungarische ausgleich, 1867,* ed. Ludovit Holitik. Bratislava: Slovak Academy, 1971.

———. "Supply and Demand for Money in Canada." In *Varieties of Monetary Experience,* ed. David Meiselman. Chicago: University of Chicago Press, 1971: 249–96.

———. *Geldpolitik in einem gemeinsamen europäischen markt* (Money in a common market setting). Baden-Baden: Nomos Verlagsgesellschaft, 1972.

———. *The International Monetary Economy and the Third World.* New York: Praeger, 1981. Chaps. 1–2.

———. *The Politics of Monetarism: Its Historical and Institutional Development.* Totowa, N.J.: Rowman and Allanheld, 1984: 16–38.

———. *Economic Nationalism and Stability.* New York: Praeger, 1985.

_____. *Monetary Policy and Rational Expectations*. New York: Praeger, 1987.

_____. "Money and a Common Market: Lessons from an Early American Experience." In *Problemi privrednog razvoja i privrednog sistems jugoslavije* (Problems of economic development and the economic system of Yugoslavia), ed. Dragomir Vojnic, Zvonimir Baletic, and Ante Cicin-Sain, et al. Zagreb: Globus, 1989: 410–23.

_____. *Money and Democracy*. New York: Praeger, 1990.

Macesich, George., ed., with the assistance of R. Lang, L. Markovic, and D. Vojnic. *Yugoslavia in the age of Democracy: Essays on Economic and Political Reform*. New York: Praeger, forthcoming.

Macesich, George, with Rikard Lang and Dragomir Vojnic, eds. *Essays on the Political Economy of Yugoslavia*. Zagreb: Informator, 1982.

_____. *Essays on the Yugoslav Economic Model*. New York: Praeger, 1989.

Macesich, George, and Charles T. Stewart, Jr. "Recent Department of Labor Studies of Minimum Wage Effects." *Southern Economic Journal* (April 1960).

Macesich, George, and Dimitrije Dimitrijevic. *Money and Finance in Contemporary Yugoslavia*. Foreword by Milton Friedman. New York: Praeger, 1973.

_____. *Money and Finance in Contemporary Yugoslavia: A Comparative Analysis*. New York: Praeger, 1984.

Malthus, Thomas R. *Essay on the Principle of Population as It Affects the Future Improvement of Society*. 1798.

_____. *Definitions on Political Economy Preceded by the Rules Which Ought to Guide Political Economists in the Definition and Use of the Terms with Remarks on the Deviation from These Rules in Their Writings*. 1827.

Marc, James G., and Herbert A. Simon. *Organizations*. New York: Wiley, 1958.

Marshall, Alfred. *Principles of Economics*. London: Macmillan, 1930.

Marx, Karl. *Das Kapital*. 1948.

Meade, James. *Problems of Economic Union*. Chicago: University of Chicago Press, 1953.

Menger, Carl (1840–1921). *Problems of Economics and Sociology*. Urbana: University of Illinois, 1963.

Mises, Ludwig von. *The Anti-Capitalistic Mentality*. New York: D. Van Nostrand, 1956.

Mitrany, David. *The Effect of the War in Southeastern Europe*. New Haven: Yale University Press, 1936.

Nasar, Sylvia. "Privatization: If you Can't Sell It, Give It Away." *U.S. News and World Report* (October 1, 1990): 73.

Nelson, Charles R. "Adjustment Lags versus Information Lags: A Test of Alternative Explanations of the Phillips Curve Phenomenon." *Journal of Money, Credit, and Banking* (February 1981): 1–11.

Peterson, John M. "Recent Needs in Minimum Wage Theory." *Southern Economic Journal* (July 1962).

Pope John Paul II. *Laborem Exercens* (On human work). 1981.

Pope Leo XIII. *Rerum Novarum* (On conditions of labor). 1891.

Pope Pius XI. *Quadragesimo Anno.* 1931.

Powell, Ellis T. *The Evolution of the Money Market, 1385–1915.* London: Frank Cass, 1966.

Reynolds, L. G. "Wages and Employment in the Labor-Surplus Economy." *American Economic Review* (March 1965).

Ricardo, David. *The High Rise of Bullion: A Proof of the Depreciation of Bank Notes.* 1810.

Rogin, L. *The Meaning and Validity of Economic Theory.* New York: Harper & Row, 1958.

Rotuenberg, Gunther E. *The Austrian Military Border in Croatia, 1522–1747.* Urbana: University of Illinois Press, 1960.

_____. *The Military Frontier in Croatia, 1740–1881.* Chicago: University of Chicago Press, 1966.

Rourke, Francis E. *Bureaucracy, Politics, and Public Policy.* 2d ed. Boston: Little, Brown, 1976.

Samuels, Warren J. "Adam Smith and the Economy as a System of Power." *Review of Social Economy* (October 1973): 123–37.

Samuelson, Paul. "Sympathy from the Other Cambridge." *The Economist* (June 25, 1983): 19–21.

Sargent, T. J., and N. Wallace. "Rational Expectations, the Optimal Monetary Instrument, and the Optimal Money Supply Rule." *Journal of Political Economy* 83 (1975): 241–54.

Say, Jean-Baptiste. *Treatise on Political Economy.* 1803.

Schumpeter, J. A. *History of Economic Analysis.* New York: Oxford University Press, 1954.

Schwartz, Anna J. *A Century of British Market Interest Rates 1874–1975.* London: The City University, 1981.

_____. "The U.S. Gold Commission and the Resurgence of Interest in a Return to the Gold Standard." *Proceedings and Reports.* Vol. 17. Tallahassee: Center for Yugoslav-American Studies, Research, and Exchanges, Florida State University, 1983.

Seidman, Harold. *Politics, Position, and Power: The Dynamics of Federal Organization.* 3d ed. New York: Oxford University Press, 1980.

Shafer, B. C. *Faces of Nationalism.* New York: Harcourt Brace Jovanovich, 1972.

Shaw, George B., ed. *Fabian Essays.* 1889.

Simmel, Georg. *The Philosophy of Money*, trans. T. Bottomore and D. Frisby, with introduction by D. Frisby. London and Boston: Routledge and Kegan Paul, 1977–1978.

Simon, Herbert A. *Administrative Behavior.* 3d ed. New York: Free Press, 1976.

Smith, Adam. *The Wealth of Nations.* 1776.

Snyder, Louis L. *The Dynamics of Nationalism.* Princeton, N.J.: Van Nostrand, 1964.

_____. *Varieties of Nationalism: A Comparative Study.* Hinsdale, Ill.: Dryden Press, 1976.

Solo, Robert A. "The New-Marxist Theory of the State." *Journal of Economic Issues* 12 (December 1978): 829–42.

_____. *The Positive State.* Cincinnati: South-Western Publishing, 1982.

Spengler, J. J., and W. R. Allen. *Essays in Economic Thought.* Chicago: Rand McNally, 1960.

_____. *Origins of Economic Thought and Justice.* Carbondale and Edwardsville: Southern Illinois University, 1980.

Stigler, George. *Production and Distribution Theories.* New York: Macmillan, 1941.

Streeten, *Paul. Economic Integration: Aspects and Problems.* Leyden, Holland: A. W. Sythoff, 1961.

Tavalas, George. "Some Initial Formulations of the Monetary Growth-Rate Rule." *History of Political Economy* (Winter 1977): 525–47.

Tawney, Richard. *The Acquisition Society.* 1920.

_____. *Religion and the Rise of Capitalism.* 1926.

_____. *Equality.* 1931.

Thornton, Henry. *Inquiry into the Nature and Effects of the Paper Credit of Great Britain.* 1802.

Tocqueville, Alexis de. *Democracy in America.* Garden City, N.Y.: Doubleday, 1969.

Veblen, Thorstein. *The Theory of the Leisure Class.* 1899.

_____. *The Theory of Business Enterprise.* 1904.

Vickers, D. *Studies in the Theory of Money, 1790–1776.* Philadelphia: Chilton, 1959.

Viner, Jacob. *Studies in the Theory of International Trade.* New York: Harper and Bros., 1937.

_____. *The Customs Union Issue.* New York: Carnegie Endowment for International Peace, 1950.

Vojnic, Dragomir. *Opca Kriza Socijalizma—Krah Boljesevicke Opcije—I Razvoj Modela Trzisne Demokracije* (General crisis of socialism—collapse of the bolshevist option—development of the market democracy). Zagreb: Ekonomski Institut, 1990.

Walker, David B. *Toward a Functioning Federalism*. Cambridge, Mass.: Winthrop, 1981.

Warwick, Donald P. *A Theory of Public Bureaucracy*. Cambridge, Mass.: Harvard University Press, 1975.

Weber, Max. *On Charisma and Institution Building—Selected Papers*, ed. and introduction by S. M. Eisenstadt. Chicago: University of Chicago Press, 1968.

Whittaker, E. *Schools and Streams of Economic Thought*. Chicago: Rand McNally, 1961.

Wildavsky, Aaron. *The Politics of the Budgetary Process*. 2d ed. Boston: Little, Brown, 1974.

Wilson, James Q. "The Rise of the Bureaucratic State." *The Public Interest* 41 (Fall 1975): 77–103.

Yaeger, Leland B., ed. *In Search of a Monetary Constitution*. Cambridge, Mass.: Harvard University Press, 1962.

Znaniecki, F. *Modern Nationalities: A Sociological Study*. Urbana: University of Illinois Press, 1952.

Index

ABOUT THE AUTHOR

GEORGE MACESICH is professor of economics and founding director of the Center for Yugoslav-American Studies, Research, and Exchanges at Florida State University, Tallahassee. In addition, he is an editorial consultant for several domestic and foreign professional journals, founding editor of *Proceedings and Reports*, and author of over twenty-five books, including *Monetary Policy and Rational Expectations* (Praeger, 1987); *Monetary Reform and Cooperation Theory* (Praeger, 1989); *Money and Democracy* (Praeger, 1990); *World Debt and Stability* (Praeger, 1991); *Money Supply Process: A Comparative Study*, with D. Dimitrijevic (Praeger, 1991); and *Yugoslavia in the Age of Democracy: Essays on Economic and Political Reform*, with R. Lang, L. Markovic, and D. Vojnic (Praeger, forthcoming).